Karen Brown's

S0-ARM-934

ENGLAND

Charming Bed & Breakfasts

Written by
JUNE BROWN

Illustrations by Barbara Tapp
Cover Painting by Jann Pollard

Karen Brown's Guides, San Mateo, California

Karen Brown Titles

Austria: Charming Inns & Itineraries

California: Charming Inns & Itineraries

England: Charming Bed & Breakfasts

England, Wales & Scotland: Charming Hotels & Itineraries

France: Charming Bed & Breakfasts

France: Charming Inns & Itineraries

Germany: Charming Inns & Itineraries

Ireland: Charming Inns & Itineraries

Italy: Charming Bed & Breakfasts

Italy: Charming Inns & Itineraries

Portugal: Charming Inns & Itineraries

Spain: Charming Inns & Itineraries

Switzerland: Charming Inns & Itineraries

Dedicated with All My Love
to My Parents
Gladys & George

Editors: Karen Brown, June Brown, Clare Brown, Iris Sandilands, Lorena Aburto.

Illustrations: Barbara Tapp; Cover painting: Jann Pollard; Web designer: Lynn Upthagrove.

Maps: Susanne Lau Alloway—Greenleaf Design & Graphics; Inside cover photo: W. Russell Ohlson.

Copyright © 1988, 1993, 1995, 1996, 1997, 1998, 1999, 2000 by Karen Brown's Guides.

This book or parts thereof may not be reproduced in any form without obtaining written permission from the publisher: Karen Brown's Guides, P.O. Box 70, San Mateo, CA 94401, USA, email: karen@karenbrown.com.

Distributed by Fodor's Travel Publications, Inc., 201 East 50th Street, New York, NY 10022, USA.

Distributed in Canada by Random House Canada, 2775 Matheson Boulevard. East, Mississanga, Ontario, Canada L4W4P7, phone (905) 624 0672, fax (905) 624 6217

Distributed in the United Kingdom, Ireland and Europe by Random House UK, 20 Vauxhall Bridge Road, London, SW1V 2SA, phone: 44 20 7840 4000, fax: 44 20 7840 8406.

Distributed in Australia by Random House Australia, 20 Alfred Street, Milsons Point, Sydney NSW 2061, Australia, phone: 61 2 9954 9966, fax: 61 2 9954 4562.

Distributed in New Zealand by Random House New Zealand, 18 Poland Road, Glenfield, Auckland, New Zealand, phone: 64 9 444 7197, fax: 64 9 444 7524.

Distributed in South Africa by Random House South Africa, Endulani, East Wing, 5A Jubilee Road, Parktown 2193, South Africa, phone: 27 11 484 3538, fax: 27 11 484 6180.

A catalog record for this book is available from the British Library.

Library of Congress Cataloging-in-Publication Data

Brown, June, 1949-
    Karen Brown's England : charming bed & breakfasts / written by
June Brown ; illustrations by Barbara Tapp ; cover painting by Jann
Pollard.
      p. cm. -- (Karen Brown's country inn series)
   Includes index.
   ISBN 0-930328-86-8
   1. Bed and breakfast accommodations--England Guidebooks.
2. England Guidebooks.   I. Brown, Karen 1956-   II. Title.
III. Series.
TX907.5.E54B76   2000
647.9442'03--dc21   99-15258
                                       CIP

Contents

Introduction

England: Charming Bed & Breakfasts describes special accommodations in tranquil countryside locations, picturesque villages, historic towns, and a selection of cultural cities beyond London. Interspersed with thatched cottages and grand ancestral manors are traditional pubs and guesthouses—all offering wholehearted hospitality in charming surroundings. Every place to stay is one that we have seen and enjoyed—our personal recommendation. We sincerely believe that where you lay your head each night makes the difference between a good and a great vacation. If you prefer to travel the hotel route, or are looking for itinerary suggestions, we trust you'll find just what you need in our companion guide, *England, Wales & Scotland: Charming Hotels & Itineraries.*

St. Michael's Mount

About Bed & Breakfast Travel

Every place to stay in this book has a different approach to bed and breakfast. Some households are very informal, some welcome children, and others invite you to sample gracious living, cocktails in the drawing room, billiards after dinner, and croquet on the lawn. The one thing that they have in common is a warmth of welcome. We have tried to be candid and honest in our appraisals and tried to convey each listing's special flavor so that you know what to expect and will not be disappointed. To help you appreciate and understand what to expect when staying at places in this guide, the following pointers are given in alphabetical order, not order of importance.

ANIMALS

Even if animals are not mentioned in the write-up, the chances are that there are friendly, tail-wagging dogs and sleek cats as visible members of the families. Many listings accept their guests' pets.

ARRIVAL AND DEPARTURE

Always discuss your time of arrival—hosts usually expect you to arrive around 6 pm. If you are going to arrive late or early, be certain to telephone your host. You are generally expected to leave by 10 on the morning of your departure. By and large, you are not expected to be on the premises during the day.

BATHROOMS

Not all listings have en-suite bathrooms in the bedrooms. Several have private bathrooms, which means that your facilities are located down the hall.

BEDROOMS

Beds are often made with duvets (down comforters) instead of the more traditional blankets and sheets. A double room has one double bed, a twin room has two single beds, and a family room contains one or more single beds in addition to a double bed. Zip and link beds are very popular: these are twin beds that can be zipped together (linked) to form an American queen-sized bed. American king and queen beds are not found very often.

CHILDREN

Places that welcome children state "Children welcome." The majority of listings in this guide do not "welcome" children but find they become tolerable at different ages over 5 or, more often than not, over 12. In some cases places simply do not accept children and the listing notes "Children not accepted." However, these indications of children's acceptability are not cast in stone, so, for example, if you have your heart set on staying at a listing that accepts children over 12, and you have an 8-year-old, call them, explain your situation, and they may well take you. Ideally, we would like to see all listings welcoming children and all parents remembering that they are staying in a home and doing their bit by making sure that children do not run wild.

CHRISTMAS

Several places offer Christmas getaways. If the information section indicates that the listing is open during the Christmas season, there is a very good chance that it offers a festive Christmas package.

CREDIT CARDS

Many bed and breakfasts in this guide do not accept plastic payment. If payment by credit card is accepted, it is indicated using the terms AX—American Express, MC—MasterCard, VS—Visa, or simply, all major.

DIRECTIONS

We give concise driving directions to guide you to the listing, which is often in a more out-of-the-way place than the town or village in the address. We would be very grateful if you would let us know of cases where our directions have proved inadequate.

ELECTRICITY

The voltage is 240. Most bathrooms have razor points (American-style) for 110 volts. It is recommended that overseas visitors take only dual-voltage appliances and a kit of electrical plug adapters. Often your host can loan you a hair dryer or an iron.

Castleton

Introduction—About Bed & Breakfast Travel

HANDICAP FACILITIES

At the back of the book we list all the places to stay that have ground-floor rooms or rooms specially equipped for the handicapped. Please discuss your requirements when you call your chosen place to stay to see if they have accommodation that is suitable for you.

MAPS

At the back of the book are a key map of Great Britain and six regional maps showing the location of the town or village nearest the lodging. To make it easier for you, we have divided each location map into a grid of four parts, a, b, c, and d, as indicated on each map's key. The pertinent regional map number is given at the right on the top line of each bed and breakfast's description. Our maps can be cross-referenced with those in our companion guide, *England, Wales & Scotland: Charming Hotels & Itineraries*. These maps are an artist's renderings are not intended to replace commercial maps: our suggestion is that you purchase a large-scale road atlas of England where an inch equals 10 miles. We use the Michelin Tourist and Motoring Atlas of Great Britain–1122, you can purchase it from our website *www.karenbrown.com*.

MEALS

Prices quoted always include breakfast. Breakfast is most likely to be juice, a choice of porridge (oatmeal) or cereal, followed by a plate of egg, bacon, sausage, tomatoes, and mushrooms completed by toast, marmalade, and jams—all accompanied by tea or coffee. A great many places offer evening meals, which should be requested at the time you make your reservation. You cannot expect to arrive at a bed and breakfast and receive dinner if you have not made reservations for it several days in advance. At some homes the social occasion of guests and host gathered around the dining-room table for an evening dinner party is a large part of the overall experience and many of these types of listings expect their guests to dine in. Places that do not offer evening meals are always happy to make recommendations at nearby pubs or restaurants.

RATES

Rates are those quoted to us for the 2000 summer season. We have tried to standardize rates by quoting the 2000 per person bed-and-breakfast rate based on two people occupying a room. Not all places conform, so where dinner is included we have stated this in the listing. Prices are always quoted to include breakfast, Value Added Tax (VAT), and service (if these are applicable). Please use the figures printed as a guideline and be certain to ask what the rate is at the time of booking. Prices for a single are usually higher than the per-person rates and prices for a family room are sometimes lower. Many listings offer special terms, below their normal prices, for "short breaks" of two or more nights. In several places suites are available at higher prices.

RESERVATIONS

When making your reservations, be sure to identify yourself as a "Karen Brown traveler." The hotels appreciate your visit, value their inclusion in our guide, and frequently tell us they take special care of our readers. We hear over and over again that the people who use our guides are such wonderful guests!

Reservations can be confining and usually must by guaranteed with a deposit. July and August are the busiest months so it is advisable to book in advance during this period. When making a reservation be specific as to what your needs are, such as a ground-floor room, en-suite shower, twin beds, family room, etc. Check the prices, which may well have changed from those given in the book (summer 2000). Ask what deposit to send or give your credit card number. Tell them approximately what time you intend to arrive and request dinner if you want it. Ask for a confirmation letter with brochure and map to be sent to you. There are several options for making reservations:

E-MAIL: This is our preferred way of making a reservation. If the hotel/bed and breakfast has an e-mail address, we have included it in the listing. (Always spell out the month as the English reverse the American month/day numbering system.)

FAX: If you have access to a fax machine, this is a very quick way to reach a hotel/bed and breakfast. If the place to stay has a fax, we have included the number. (See comment above about spelling out the month.)

LETTER: If you write for reservations, you will usually receive back your confirmation and a map. You should then send your deposit. (See comment under e-mail about spelling out the month.)

TELEPHONE: By telephoning you have your answer immediately, so if space is not available, you can then decide on an alternative. If calling from the United States, allow for the time difference (England is five hours ahead of New York) so that you can call during their business day. Dial 011 (the international code), 44 (England's code), then the city code (dropping the 0) and the telephone number.

Although proprietors do not always strictly adhere to it, it is important to understand that once reservations are confirmed, whether by phone or in writing, you are under contract. This means that the proprietor is legally obligated to provide the accommodation he has promised and that you are bound to pay for that accommodation. If you cannot take up your accommodation, you are liable for a portion of the accommodation charges plus your deposit. If you have to cancel your reservation, do so as soon as possible so that the proprietor can attempt to re-let your room, in which case you are liable only for the re-let fee or the deposit.

SIGHTSEEING

Since few countries have as much sightseeing to offer in a concentrated space as England, we have tried to mention major attractions near each lodging to encourage you to spend several nights in each location. Within a few miles of every listing there are places of interest to visit and explore: lofty cathedrals, quaint churches, museums, and grand country houses.

SMOKING

Nearly all listings forbid smoking either in the bedrooms or public rooms. Some allow no smoking at all, in which case we state "No-smoking house." Ask about smoking policies if this is important to you—best to be forewarned rather than frustrated.

SOCIALIZING

We have tried to indicate the degree of socializing that is included in your stay as some hosts treat their guests like visiting friends and relatives, sharing cocktails, eating with them around the dining table, and joining them for coffee after dinner (the difference being that friends and relatives do not receive a bill at the end of their stay).

Kersey

Introduction—About Bed & Breakfast Travel

WOLSEY LODGES

Several of our listings are members of Wolsey Lodges, a consortium of private houses that open their doors to a handful of guests at a time. Visitors become a part of the household—guests are not expected to scuttle up to their rooms and family life does not carry on away from guests behind closed doors. Everyone usually dines together round a polished table, and unless you make special requests, you eat what is served to you. The conversation flows and you meet those you might never have met elsewhere. Early or late in the season, you may find that you are the only guests in these houses and you can enjoy a romantic candlelit dinner in a house full of character and charm. You are welcome as guests because you are the ones who help the owners pay their central-heating bills, private school fees, and gardeners. As with all the listings in this guide, Wolsey Lodge members approach bed and breakfast in different ways—some are informal, while others offer a taste of refined, gracious living. If a lodging is a member of this group, we state "Wolsey Lodge" in the information section. A brochure listing all the Wolsey Lodge properties is available from Wolsey Lodges, 9 Market Place, Hadleigh, Ipswich, Suffolk IP7 5DL, England, tel: (01473) 822058, fax: (01473) 827444.

About England

DRIVING

Just about the time overseas visitors board their return flight home, they will have adjusted to driving on the "right" side which is the left side in England. You must contend with such things as roundabouts (circular intersections); flyovers (overpasses); ring roads (peripheral roads whose purpose is to bypass city traffic); lorries (trucks); laybys (turnouts); boots (trunks); and bonnets (hoods). Pedestrians are permitted to cross the road anywhere and always have the right of way. Seat belts must be worn at all times.

Motorways: The letter "M" precedes these convenient ways to cover long distances. With three or more lanes of traffic either side of a central divider, you should stay in the left-hand lane except for passing. Motorway exits are numbered and correspond to numbering on major road maps. Service areas supply petrol, cafeterias, and "bathrooms" (the word "bathroom" is used in the American sense—in Britain "bathroom" means a room with a shower or bathtub, not a toilet: "loo" is the most commonly used term for an American bathroom).

"A" Roads: The letter "A" precedes the road number. All major roads fall into this category. They vary from three lanes either side of a dividing barrier to single carriageways with an unbroken white line in the middle indicating that passing is not permitted. These roads have the rather alarming habit of changing abruptly from dual to single carriageway.

"B" Roads and Country Roads: The letter "B" preceding the road number or the lack of any lettering or numbering indicates that the road belongs to the maze of country roads that crisscross Britain. These are the roads for people who have the luxury of time to enjoy the scenery en route. Arm yourself with a good map (although getting lost is part of the fun). Driving these narrow roads is terrifying at first but exhilarating after a while. Meandering down these roads, you can expect to spend time crawling behind a tractor or cows being herded to the farmyard. Some lanes are so narrow that there is room for only one car.

DRIVING–CAR RENTAL

Readers frequently ask our advice on car rental companies. We always use Auto Europe, a car rental broker that works with the major car rental companies to find the lowest possible price. They also offer motor homes and chauffeur services. Auto Europe's toll-free phone service from every European country connects you to their US-based, 24-hour reservation center (ask for the card with European phone numbers to be sent to you). Auto Europe offers our readers a 5% discount, and occasionally free upgrades. Karen Brown readers can also obtain a free car phone with rentals of 7 days or more. You will be responsible for the activation fee ($30), cost to ship the phone to your home ($30), and charge for time used. Be sure to use the Karen Brown ID number 99006187 to receive your discount and any special offers. You can make your own reservations via our website, *www.karenbrown.com* (select Auto Europe from the home page under Travel Center), or by phone (1-800-223-5555).

INFORMATION

The British Tourist Authority is an invaluable source of information. You can visit their website at *www.visitbritain.org*. Its major offices are located as follows:

AUSTRALIA–SYDNEY: BTA, Level 16, Gateway, 1 Macquarie Place, Sydney NWS 2000, tel: (02) 9377-4400, fax: (02) 9377-4499

CANADA–TORONTO: BTA, 5915 Airport Road, Suite 120, Mississauga, Ontario L4V 1T1, tel: (888) VISITUK, fax: (416) 405 1835

FRANCE–PARIS: BTA, Maison de la Grand Bretagne, 19 Rue des Mathurins, 75009 Paris, tel: (1) 4451-5620, fax: (1) 4451-5621

GERMANY–FRANKFURT: BTA, Westendstrasse 16-22, 60325 Frankfurt, tel: (069) 97 112-3, fax: (069) 97 1122 444

NEW ZEALAND–AUCKLAND: BTA, Suite 305, 3rd Floor, Dilworth Building, corner Queen and Customs Streets, Auckland 1, tel: (09) 303-1446, fax: (09) 377-6965

USA–CHICAGO: BTA, 625 North Michigan Avenue, Suite 1001, Chicago, IL 60611— walk-in inquiries only

USA–NEW YORK: BTA, 551 Fifth Avenue, Suite 701, New York, NY 10176, tel: (800) 462-2748.

If you need additional information while you are in Britain, there are more than 700 official Tourist Information Centres identified by a blue-and-white letter "I" and "Tourist Information" signs. Many information centers will make reservations for local accommodation and larger ones will "book a bed ahead" in a different locality.

In London at the British Visitor Centre at 1 Regent Street, London SW1Y 4PQ (near Piccadilly Circus tube station) you can book a room, hire a car, or pay for a coach tour or theatre tickets. It is open 9 am to 6:30 pm, Monday to Friday; 10 am to 4 pm Saturday and Sunday, with extended hours from mid-May to September.

PUBS

Pubs are a British institution. Traditional pubs with inviting names such as the Red Lion, Wheatsheaf, and King's Arms are found at the heart of every village. Not only are they a great place to meet the locals over a pint or a game of dominoes or darts, but they offer an inviting place to dine. Food served in the bar enables you to enjoy an inexpensive meal while sipping your drink in convivial surroundings. Bar meals range from a bowl of soup to a delicious cooked dinner. Many pubs have dining rooms that serve more elaborate fare in equally convivial but more sophisticated surroundings. The key to success when dining at a pub is to obtain a recommendation from where you are staying that night—your host is always happy to assist you.

SHOPPING

Non-EU members can reclaim the VAT (Value Added Tax) paid on the goods they purchase. Not all stores participate in the refund scheme and there is often a minimum purchase price. Stores that do participate will ask to see your passport before completing the VAT form. This form must be presented with the goods to the Customs officer at the point of departure from Britain within three months of purchase. The customs officer will certify the form. After having the receipts validated by customs you can receive a refund in cash from the tax-free refund counter. Alternatively, you can mail your validated receipts to the store where you bought the goods. The store will then send you a check in sterling for the refund.

SIGHTSEEING

There is so much to see in every little nook and cranny of England: cottage gardens, Roman ruins, stately homes, thatched villages, ancient castles, Norman churches, smugglers' inns, bluebell woods, historic manors, museums on every subject. All set in a land that moves from wild moorland to verdant farmland, woodland to meadow, vast sandy beaches to rugged cliffs. Most sightseeing venues operate a summer and a winter opening schedule, the changeover occurring around late March/early April and late October/early November. Before you embark on an excursion, check the dates and hours of opening. The British Tourist Authority is an invaluable resource for what to see and do in an area. Our companion guide, *England, Wales & Scotland: Charming Hotels & Itineraries,* includes countryside driving itineraries which are useful in helping you plan your holiday.

WEATHER

Britain has a tendency to be moist at all times of the year. The cold in winter is rarely severe; however, the farther north you go, the greater the possibility of being snowed in. Spring can be wet, but it is a lovely time to travel—the summer crowds have not descended, daffodils and bluebells fill the woodlands, and the hedgerows are full of wildflowers. Summer offers the best chance of sunshine, but also the largest crowds. Schools are usually closed the last two weeks of July and all of August, so this is the time when most families take their summer holidays. Travel is especially hectic on the weekends in summer—try to avoid major routes and airports at these times. Autumn is also an ideal touring time. The weather tends to be drier than in spring and the woodlands are decked in their golden autumn finery.

Bed & Breakfast Descriptions

The Benedictine monks chose a magnificent site high on a hill overlooking the sea to found their Abbey of St. Peter in 1024. Despite having been sacked by Henry VIII and burned by Cromwell, a lot of the monastic settlement remains: the church, the magnificent swannery, an enormous thatched tithe barn, a ruined watermill, and most importantly the infirmary. Now home to the Cookes, the infirmary was originally a resting-place for visitors, evolving over the years into a farmhouse and now a welcoming guesthouse and tea-room. Pink chairs with tables topped with pink cloths are set around the giant inglenook fireplace in the old kitchen. Breakfast and lunch are served here or, on warm summer days, under the vine-covered arbor or on the lawn overlooking the barn. Bedrooms range in size from a spacious suite with a sitting room and separate bedroom to a cottagey little room set beneath the eaves and reached by a narrow staircase. The adjacent tithe barn contains interesting exhibits while the farm with its array of animals is a great attraction to young visitors as is the nearby swannery with its vast colony of swans. Abbotsbury is a delightful village of thatched houses very typical of those found just a short drive away in Hardy country, a favorite destination for visitors. *Directions*: Abbotsbury is midway between Weymouth and Bridport on the B3157. In Abbotsbury turn towards the sea (signposted The Swannery) and Abbey House is on your left after 100 yards.

ABBEY HOUSE
Owners: Maureen & Jonathan Cooke
Church Street
Abbotsbury
Dorset DT3 4JJ, England
Tel: (01305) 871330, Fax: (01305) 871088
www.karenbrown.com/england/abbeyhouse.html
5 rooms, 4 en suite
£32.50–£35 per person
Open all year, Credit cards: none
Children welcome, No-smoking house

Pam and David Veen run this impressive house, built as a vicarage in 1869, as a small hotel, providing a centrally located, comfortable, hospitable base for exploring the Lake District. Pamela decorated the house with antiques and bric-a-brac, creating interesting corners to relax and enjoy the tranquility that premeates this lovely old house. Most of the bedrooms have antique or four-poster beds with views across the river to the distant mountains. All have antique pictures and porcelain, crisp white sheets, and patchwork quilts. Accommodation can be taken on a bed-and-breakfast basis, but guests usually opt to include dinner because Pamela makes every effort to make this meal a special occasion. Grey Friar Lodge is just a short distance from the bustling center of Ambleside. Whether you explore Lakeland by car or on foot, you will find the scenery glorious: in spring the famous daffodils bloom, while in autumn the bracken and leaves turn a crisp, golden brown. At nearby Grasmere are Rydal Mount and Dove Cottage, poet William Wordsworth's homes. Hawkshead has a museum honoring Beatrix Potter and in Near Sawrey you can visit her home, Hill Top Farm, where she dreamed up such endearing characters as Mrs. Tiggy Winkle and the Flopsy Bunnies. *Directions:* Grey Friar Lodge is 1½ miles west of Ambleside on the A593 (Coniston road), midway between Ambleside and Skelwith Bridge.

GREY FRIAR LODGE
Owners: Pam & David Veen
Clappersgate, Ambleside
Cumbria LA22 9NE, England
Tel & fax: (015394) 33158
E-mail: greyfriar@veen.freeserve.co.uk
www.karenbrown.com/england/greyfriarlodge.html
8 rooms, 7 en suite
£27.50–£42.50 per person, dinner £17.50
Open Mar to Oct
Credit cards: MC, VS
Children over 12, No-smoking house

The Barns is a comfortable spot to break a long journey between London and Edinburgh via the A1, or for a longer visit to explore Nottinghamshire. This county is famous not only for the exploits of Robin Hood, but also as the area where the Pilgrim Fathers formed their separatist church before setting sail for America and establishing a new colony. The Barns was very tastefully converted from the hay and tractor barns of the next-door farm, and behind its red-brick façade all is spick-and-span. A sofa and chairs are drawn around a crackling log fire, and tables are topped with linen cloths neatly laid for breakfast. Upstairs, the bedrooms are plainly decorated with cream walls highlighting dark beams and all have nice touches such as a fresh posy of flowers on a small antique dresser and elegant china teacups (one ground-floor room is also available). Rooms 1 and 5 are particularly large, more luxurious rooms. A pleasant drive through Sherwood Forest brings you to the visitors' center which has an exhibition on Robin Hood and his merry band and offers maps guiding you through ancient oak trees to his former hideaways. Clumber Park near Sherwood Forest is noted for its main driveway planted with over 1,296 lime trees. *Directions:* From the south take the A1 north to the A57 (Worksop) roundabout, make a U turn and go south on the A1. Take the first left, on the B6420, towards Retford. The Barns is on the left after 2 miles.

THE BARNS
Owners: Mary & Harry Kay
Morton Farm, Babworth, Retford
Nottinghamshire DN22 8HA, England
Tel: (01777) 706336, Fax: (01777) 709773
www.karenbrown.com/england/thebarns.html
6 rooms
£24–£40 per person
Open all year
Credit cards: all major
Children welcome
No-smoking house

On a road of large, semi-detached Edwardian homes, Haydon House distinguishes itself as having the most colorful, pocket-sized garden. Magdalene has made the most of her home, decorating each of the rooms to perfection. Guests enjoy the sitting room with its plump sofas drawn cozily round the fire or the pocket-sized study with just enough room to spread your maps and books to plan the next day's adventures. The bedrooms are exceedingly pretty and named for the color of their decor: Strawberry, Gooseberry, Blueberry, Elderberry, and Mulberry. Request Blueberry or Elderberry if you want a more spacious room. Mulberry, tucked under the eaves, is an especially attractive triple or family room. With a choice of over 90 restaurants in the town, breakfast is the only meal served and includes a fresh-fruit platter and several other alternatives to a traditional, cooked English breakfast. Bath with its graceful, honey-colored buildings, interesting museums, and superb shopping merits several days' exploration. *Directions:* From Bath follow signs onto the A367 towards Exeter, pass an elongated roundabout by a railway viaduct, go up a hill to a small shopping area, and onto a dual carriageway (The Bear pub is on your right). At the end of the shops fork right into Bloomfield Road and take the second right (by the telephone kiosk) into Bloomfield Park.

HAYDON HOUSE
Owners: Magdalene & Gordon Ashman-Marr
9 Bloomfield Park
Bath
Somerset BA2 2BY, England
Tel & fax: (01225) 444919 & 427351
E-mail: stay@haydonhouse.co.uk
www.karenbrown.com/england/haydonhouse.html
5 rooms
£35–£45 per person
Open all year
Credit cards: all major
Children welcome
No-smoking house

Perched high above the city's rooftops, this large Victorian home offers every comfort to the visitor: luxurious bathrooms with heated towel rails and perfect showers, firm, American queen-sized beds, satellite television, in-house movies, picture-perfect decor, and the sincere attentions of George. Each of the bedrooms has its own flavor and, while I admired those in soft flowery pastels (the pink tower room with its lacy four-poster bed is very popular with honeymooners and there is a spacious ground-floor room for those who have difficulty with stairs), I particularly enjoyed the imaginative four-poster room where four turquoise obelisks are artfully draped in navy-and-white fabric to form the - posts of this most interesting bed. Breakfast in the sunny green and yellow breakfast room offers lots of choices as well as the traditional English cooked breakfast. It's a 15-minute walk into town. George has designed driving tours with detailed instructions for a full day's sightseeing, so guests often venture as far afield as southern Wales. *Directions:* From Bath follows signs onto the A367 towards Exeter, pass an elongated roundabout by a railway viaduct, go up a hill, and take the first turning to the right into Upper Oldfield Park. Holly Lodge is the first house on the right just past the bend.

HOLLY LODGE
Owner: George Hall
8 Upper Oldfield Park
Bath
Somerset BA2 3JZ, England
Tel: (01225) 424042, Fax: (01225) 481138
E-mail: stay@hollylodge.co.uk
www.karenbrown.com/england/hollylodge.html
7 rooms
£42–£47 per person
Open all year
Credit cards: all major
Children welcome
No-smoking house

Situated halfway up a steep hill, Somerset House is a classic Regency abode of warm, honey-colored stone, set in a spacious garden affording panoramic views of the city. The family pets along with family photos and books give a comfortable feeling to the Seymours' upscale guesthouse. Decorated in pastels, the bedrooms have matching drapes and bedspreads and whimsical rag dolls propped up on the pillows. Several rooms have an extra bed and a ground-floor room is ideal for those who have difficulty with stairs. Bedrooms are named after the sons and daughters of George III and in their note to guests Jean and Malcolm have included the child's historical particulars as well as the rules of the house. Jean and Jonathan specialize in delicious regional English cuisine. Saturday nights (not in the summer) are particularly special, for Jean plans a theme meal (on the night of our stay it was France) and gives a verbal rendition of the menu, explaining the origins of the dishes and their tempting contents. The basement dining room complements the food, with light-wood Windsor chairs, lace-topped tables, and a huge pine dresser set upon the checkerboard tile floor. A 12-minute walk brings you into the heart of Bath. *Directions:* Do not go into the city center, but follow signs for the university. Going up Bathwick Hill, Somerset House is on the left.

SOMERSET HOUSE
Owners: Jean, Malcolm & Jonathan Seymour
35 Bathwick Hill
Bath
Somerset BA2 6LD, England
Tel: (01225) 466451, Fax: (01225) 317188
E-mail: somersethouse@compuserve.com
www.karenbrown.com/england/somersethouse.html
10 rooms, 9 en suite
£35.50 per person, dinner £19.50
Open all year
Credit cards: all major
Children over 6, No-smoking house

Rosamund and John Napier were delighted to find this lovely Georgian House on a quiet street in the conservation village of Bathford just 3 miles from Bath. It was just what they had been looking for—a large home, suitable for bed and breakfast. Over the years they have added bathrooms and showers, decorated and slowly added antique furniture. It's more comfortably homey than decorator-perfect, with the Napiers' warmth of welcome adding the final ingredient. The spacious sitting room overlooks the grassy garden with its tennis court and guests help themselves to drinks at the honesty bar. Upstairs, the larger bedrooms can be easily adapted to include an extra bed or two for children who just pay for breakfast if sharing their parents' room. Each room is well equipped with color TV, phone, tea-making facilities, hair dryer, and en-suite shower or bathroom. If you would like complete privacy, opt to stay in one of the bedrooms in the walled garden cottage. Bathford is ideally situated for Bath (there are three buses an hour) and within easy reach of Bradford on Avon, Lacock, Longleat House, Stourhead Gardens, Bowood House, and Dyrham Park. *Directions:* From Bath take the A4 towards Chippenham for 3 miles, the A363 towards Bradford on Avon for 100 yards, then turn left up Bathford Hill. Church Street is the first right and Eagle House is on your right after 200 yards.

EAGLE HOUSE
Owners: Rosamund & John Napier
Church Street
Bathford, near Bath
Somerset BA1 7RS, England
Tel: (01225) 859946, Fax: (01225) 859430
E-mail: jonap@eagleho.demon.co.uk
www.karenbrown.com/england/eaglehouse.html
8 rooms
£28–£38 per person
Closed Christmas & New Year
Credit cards: MC, VS
Children welcome

Frog Street Farm, a lovely gray-stone farmhouse dating back to 1436, is a real working farm where things are not fancy or cutesy-pretty, but everything fits together perfectly with country freshness. From the moment you are met at the door by Veronica, with her true country-style warmth and jolly sense of humor, the mood is set. You are immediately made to feel part of the family and offered a cup of tea in front of the large inglenook fireplace before being shown to your room. The guestrooms are spotlessly clean and simply, but prettily decorated throughout with a color scheme of pinks and greens. Behind the house lies the farmyard, while to the front is a colorful garden and a swimming pool shaded by a tall hedge. Veronica takes great pride in her cooking and, with advance notice, will prepare delicious meals from farm-fresh produce. For those who want to spend a few days in the country, away from city sophistication, Frog Street Farm is the epitome of what a farm vacation should be. In this pretty, rolling countryside are the charming little towns of Chard, Ilchester, Ilminster, and Crewkerne. To the north the limestone Mendip Hills are honeycombed with spectacular caves and gorges such as Wookey Hole and Cheddar Gorge. The magnificent cathedral city of Wells is within easy driving distance. *Directions:* From the M5 take exit 25 and continue 4½ miles southeast to Hatch Beauchamp. Take Station Road to Frog Street Farm.

FROG STREET FARM
Owners: Veronica & Henry Cole
Beercrocombe
Taunton
Somerset TA3 6AF, England
Tel & fax: (01823) 480430
3 rooms
£25–£30 per person, dinner £17
Open Apr to Oct
Credit cards: none
Children over 11, No-smoking house

Set in a luxuriant garden, this 14th-century thatched Dartmoor longhouse, one of only a handful remaining, presents an idyllic picture. Guests are welcomed with tea on the lawn in summer and immediately made to feel at home. The house has lots of charming features such as enormous granite fireplaces, sloping walls, low doors, exposed beams, and low, often sloping ceilings. The three small double bedrooms at the top of the steep, narrow staircase are cottage-cozy, each with a double four-poster bed which hugs the ceiling. Two bedrooms have snug en-suite shower rooms while the third has its shower across the hall. There are many old and characterful pubs and restaurants nearby for dinner. Tor Down House is in Dartmoor National Park and a short walk up the lane finds you amidst the bracken and climbing up to the rugged tors. Gardens are popular with visitors and in the next village is one featuring the national collection of hostas. Rosemoor, the Royal Horticultural Society garden, is also nearby. An ideal base offering easy access to the West Country. *Directions:* Leave the A30 at the junction signposted Okehampton and Belstone (there are two Okehampton junctions). Follow signs for Belstone (2 miles) and in the center of the village take the lane that turns right immediately after the post office. You find Tor Down House's wooden five-bar gate after ¾ mile, soon after crossing the cattle grid.

TOR DOWN HOUSE
Owners: Maureen & John Pakenham
Belstone, Okehampton
Devon EX20 1QY, England
Tel & fax: (01837) 840731 (phone to arrange to fax)
www.karenbrown.com/england/tordownhouse.html
3 rooms, 2 en suite
£30 per person
Closed Christmas & New Year
Credit cards: MC, VS
Children over 14
No-smoking house

Middle Ord Manor is the most spacious of homes, built over 200 years ago as the landowner's residence for the Grey family. There have always been Greys here, though Geoffrey and Joan are not relations. They are the first to spell their name with an "a" and the first to farm the estate rather than supervise it. Joan has a welcoming way with guests and has packed a table in the spacious upstairs sitting room with enough information to keep you busy for a fortnight. The spacious bedrooms are kitted out with every extra, from a trouser press to homemade biscuits. The beds—a queen four-poster, twins, and a king—are comfortable and each room has its own shower room. For those who wish to take a bath, there is an additional bathroom. Breakfast is the only meal served but Joan has all the menus of local eateries on hand so that guests can choose one that fits their fancy and their pocketbook. Nearby Berwick is a historic town within two sets of walls. You reach nearby Lindisfarne (Holy Island) by a causeway from the mainland at low tide and Joan has a tide table showing the safe crossing times. Lindisfarne mead is made there and the factory is open to the public. Bamburgh, Alnwick, and Floors Castles are all close at hand. *Directions:* Remain on the A1 bypass around Berwick-upon-Tweed and take the A689 signposted Cornhill for ¼ mile. At the small fingerpost sign on your right, turn left for Middle Ord and follow the lane to the house.

MIDDLE ORD MANOR
Owners: Joan & Geoffrey Gray
Middle Ord
Berwick-upon-Tweed
Northumberland TD15 2XQ, England
Tel: (01289) 306323, Fax: (01289) 308423
E-mail: joan@middleord.freeserve.co.uk
www.karenbrown.com/england/middleord.html
3 rooms
£27 per person
Open Easter to October, Credit cards: none
Children over 16, No-smoking house

This well-proportioned Victorian rectory is set in secluded grounds overlooking glorious vistas of the Derbyshire countryside. Geraldine and Stuart Worthington's solicitous welcome includes an invitation to the evening dinner party. Guests are introduced to each other over cocktails in the drawing room before sitting down at the large dining-room table, beautifully laid with silver and crystal. Geraldine and Stuart dine with their guests, Geraldine serving unobtrusively, with Stuart pouring the wine. After dinner, guests, host, and hostess return to the drawing room for port and coffee around the cheery log fire. The front bedroom has a large double bed framed by blue-and-white flowered draperies hung from a coronet, matching bedspread and bed ruffle, and an en-suite shower room. The large twin room has thick bathrobes so guests can pop comfortably across the hall to their bathroom. The third twin room tucked under the eaves has a steeply sloping ceiling and adjacent luxurious shower room. The dramatic and rugged Derbyshire scenery is a strong attraction for walkers. Many visitors also tour Chatsworth House, Haddon Hall, and the open-air Monday market in Bakewell. *Directions:* Leave Ashbourne on the A52 towards Leek. After 2 miles turn right towards Ilam. Drive through Okeover Park and turn left as you go through the gates. After 2 miles, at Blore crossroads, turn left and The Old Rectory is on your right beyond the church.

THE OLD RECTORY
Owners: Geraldine & Stuart Worthington
Blore, Ashbourne
Derbyshire DE6 2BS, England
Tel & fax: (01335) 350287
www.karenbrown.com/england/theoldrectory.html
3 rooms, 1 en suite
£40 per person, dinner £22.50
Closed Christmas
Credit cards: MC, VS
Children over 15
Wolsey Lodge

Kath and Tony Peacock live in what was Boltongate's large, rambling rectory that dates from 1360 but was extensively "modernized" in Victorian times. Many of its rooms face south and have delightful views of peaceful countryside with distant views of the Lakeland fells and mountains. In summer the sun streams in and guests can enjoy the garden with its ponds and arbors, while during the cooler months log fires burn in the study and dining room. Dining in the cozy oak-beamed dining room is a delightful experience. In contrast to the old-world dining room, the bedrooms and sitting room are spacious and tall-ceilinged, large windowed rooms. Bedrooms are large and comfortable, decorated with pretty wallpapers and matching drapes. Two have en-suite bathrooms while the largest has its bathroom (robes provided) down the hall. Boltongate is on the quiet, northernmost fringes of the Lake District, a perfect spot to break a journey to or from Scotland. Pretty towns and villages such as Caldbeck, Borrowdale, Ullswater, and Buttermere abound. William Wordsworth's birthplace is nearby in Cockermouth. *Directions:* From the Keswick bypass take the A591 for 7 miles. At the Castle Inn turn right at the sign for Ireby. Drive through Ireby to Boltongate (1½ miles). The Rectory is the first house on the right as you come up the hill.

BOLTONGATE OLD RECTORY
Owners: Kathleen & Anthony Peacock
Boltongate
Cumbria CA5 1DA, England
Tel: (016973) 71647, Fax: (016973) 71798
E-mail: boltongate@aol.com
www.karenbrown.com/england/boltongateoldrectory.html
3 rooms, 2 en suite
£37–£38 per person, dinner £23
Closed Christmas & New Year
Credit cards: MC, VS
Children over 14
No-smoking house
Wolsey Lodge

Priory Steps, a row of 17th-century weavers' cottages high above the town of Bradford on Avon, is a glorious place to stay. The village tumbles down the hill to the banks of the River Avon, its narrow streets full of interesting shops and antique dealers. A few miles distant, the glories of Bath await exploration and are easily accessible by car or the local train service. Hostess Diana is a gourmet cook and guests dine *en famille* in the traditionally furnished dining room. While Diana's cooking is reason enough to spend several days here, the adjacent library with its books and pamphlets highlighting the many places to visit in the area provides additional justification. The bedrooms are all very different, each accented with antique furniture, and each has a smart modern bathroom, television, and tea and coffee tray. The Blue Room has large shuttered and curtained windows and a pleasing decor in shades of blue and pink, while the large English Room has striped paper in muted tones of green coordinating with flowered curtains. There is a touch of whimsy in the bathroom of the dark-beamed Frog Room where an odd frog or two has inspired former guests to send their own contributions to an ever-growing collection of the creatures. The frogless bedroom itself is very pretty. *Directions:* Take the A363 from Bath to Bradford on Avon. As the road drops steeply into the town, Newtown is the first road to the right. Priory Steps is 150 yards on the left.

PRIORY STEPS
Owners: Diana & Carey Chapman
Newtown
Bradford on Avon
Wiltshire BA15 1NQ, England
Tel: (01225) 862230, Fax: (01225) 866248
E-mail: priorysteps@clara.co.uk
www.karenbrown.com/england/priorysteps.html
5 rooms
£35–£39 per person, dinner £20
Open all year, Credit cards: MC, VS
Children over 12, Wolsey Lodge

After years of having a home both in England and Canada, Barbara and Barrie decided to settle in England and found the perfect house in this gracious Georgian home in Brampford Speke, a delightful little village just outside Exeter. Guests use the large drawing room, which opens up to the spacious conservatory where Barbara serves breakfast. Upstairs are two very attractive bedrooms each accompanied by a dressing room and large bathroom. For those traveling with children an additional bedroom can be combined with one of the bedrooms to make a private family suite. For dinner, guests often walk to the nearby Agricultural Inn, which serves good pub food as well as having an excellent restaurant, and Barbara has a list of recommended pubs and restaurants farther afield. Jane Austen is supposed to have based her novel *Sense and Sensibility* hereabouts and Barbara will direct you to the nearby spots featured in the book. From here you can visit the north and south Devon coasts while closer at hand is Dartmoor with its villages nestled in green valleys with the moor high above. It's an ideal place to stay if you are attending the Exeter music festival, which takes place for three weeks in July. *Directions:* From Exeter take the A377 towards Crediton. After passing over the Exe bridge on the outskirts of town turn right to Brampford Speke and Brampford House is on the left in the village, just beyond the church and before the red telephone box.

BRAMPFORD HOUSE
Owners: Barbara & Barrie Smith
Brampford Speke, nr Exeter
Devon EX 5DW, England
Tel: (01392) 841195, Fax (01392) 841196
www.karenbrown.com/england/brampfordhouse.html
3 rooms, 2 en-suite
£22–£35 per person
Open Mar to Oct
Credit cards: none
Children over 8
No-smoking house

Gently rolling hills with sheep grazing peacefully and shaded valleys with meandering streams surround the picturesque village of Broad Campden where The Malt House hugs the quiet main street and opens up at the rear to a beautiful garden. Years ago barley was made into malt here for brewing beer. Now a picturesque, country house, it provides a perfect central location for exploring other Cotswold villages. It is very much a family operation with Nick and Jean at the front of the house and son Julian as the talented chef. Julian offers three choices for each of the three dinner courses served in the inviting dining room where an open fire blazes on chilly evenings. Of the two lounges the little sitting room with its comfortable chairs arranged round the massive inglenook fireplace and mullioned windows offering glimpses of the garden is a favorite place to relax and toast your toes by the fire in winter. The bedroom decor ranges from cottage-cozy to contemporary, and most of the immaculate bathrooms have old-fashioned tubs. Five bedrooms are in the house while an inviting ground-floor suite and two bedrooms are in the stable block. Lovely Cotswold villages to explore include Chipping Campden, Bourton-on-the-Water, Upper and Lower Slaughter, Stow-on-the-Wold, Bibury, and Broadway. Garden lovers will enjoy Kiftsgate, Hidcote Manor, and Batsford. *Directions:* On entering Chipping Campden, take the first right: you know you are in Broad Campden when you see the Bakers Arms. The Malt House is opposite the wall topped by a tall topiary hedge.

THE MALT HOUSE
Owners: Jean, Julian, & Nick Brown
Broad Campden, Chipping Campden
Gloucestershire GL55 6UU, England
Tel: (01386) 840295, Fax: (01386) 841334
E-mail: nick@the-malt-house.freeserve.co.uk
www.karenbrown.com/england/themalthouse.html
8 rooms
£48.50–£67.50 per person, dinner £28.50
Closed Christmas, Credit cards: all major
Children over 5

Barn House is a handsome, stone 17th-century house in 16 acres of paddocks and gardens, which are open to the public (monies collected are donated to a local charity). Overnight guests are privileged to enjoy the grounds and the outdoor, enclosed swimming pool as well as the home. A long and rambling large lounge with dramatic, high, arched ceiling and beams, referred to as the Great Hall, is accessed off the entry. Jane and Mark offer overnight accommodation in four large guestrooms, three with en-suite bathrooms, which are found down long, narrow hallways whose floors are covered with tapestry runners. The rooms are set behind high pine doors with brass knockers. A twin room features a picture of Mark and friend dramatically jumping in a competition; a large double room enjoys a sitting area, enormous bath, and old, exposed, pine beams; the Pink Room with a king bed and sitting area can be shared with a small double that overlooks the courtyard garden. The Garden Suite enjoys a large sitting area with TV, a bedroom with a double bed, and windows looking out across the croquet lawn to sheep fields beyond. Breakfast is served in the dining room, which is very British in decor, with colors of blues, reds, and tan. *Directions:* Broadway is off the A44 between Evesham and Stow-on-the-Wold. Drive through town on High Street with the Lygon Arms on the left, and Barn House is just a few blocks farther, past the shops on the same side of the street.

*BARN HOUSE   **New***
Owners: Jane & Mark Ricketts
152 High Street
Broadway
Worcestershire WR12 7AJ, England
Tel & fax: (01386) 858633
E-mail: barnhouse@btinternet.com
4 rooms, 3 en suite
£25 per person
Open all year, Credit cards: none
Children welcome

A handsome gold-on-blue sign advertising bed and breakfast accommodation caught our attention soon after we left Broadway and tempted us down a country lane. The next sign, "Drive Slowly—Free Range Children and Animals" made us chuckle, so we stopped to look around. With Sue Adams looking for something to occupy her time now that her children require less attention, her husband, Mike, converted the central section of their home to accommodate overnight guests. Three comfortably sized guestrooms are fresh in their newness and pretty in their decor of light-pine furniture against cream walls. Two rooms are found on either side of the entry and the third is tucked under the angled roofline. While guests do not have a sitting room, they sometimes settle in the evening at the tables in the breakfast room where a library of books is available to browse through and views look out to the surrounding greenery. The Adams ask that guests not use the deck directly behind the home as this is established as their private family area, but guests can relax on the front flagstone terrace. At the edge of the property trails lead down to the fields and along the Cotswold Way. *Directions:* Travel the A44 east from Broadway and just before the intersection for Chipping Campden, look for their sign on the right stating "Country House B&B."

HIGHLANDS COUNTRY HOUSE   **New**
Owners: Susan & Mike Adams
Fish Hill
Broadway
Worcestershire WR12 7LD, England
Tel: (01386) 858015, Fax: (01386) 852584
E-mail: sue@adames.demon.co.uk
3 rooms
£25 per person
Closed December
Credit cards: none
Children welcome
No-smoking house

Broadway with its attractive shops is one of the loveliest Cotswold villages and certainly one of the busiest. A stay at Milestone House not only gives you the opportunity to enjoy the village after the daytime crowds have left but also provides a convenient base for exploring this lovely part of the country. Like many of the houses in the village, Milestone House was built in the early part of the 17th century and is full of period charm. Guests have two comfortable sitting rooms and a large sunny conservatory where breakfast is served overlooking the garden. At dinner time guests choose from the array of eating establishments in Broadway and the surrounding villages. Up the narrow staircase you find three cottagey bedrooms. The two at the front of the house have shower rooms while a third enjoys a larger bathroom and overlooks the garden. Guests who are staying longer than a couple of nights particularly enjoy the courtyard room with its own private entrance. Doreen and Granville take lots of interest in their guests and encourage them to follow one of their driving itineraries through the off-the-beaten-track Cotswold villages. *Directions:* Broadway is off the A44 between Evesham and Stow-on-the-Wold. Milestone House is located on the High Street. There's a car park to the rear.

MILESTONE HOUSE
Owners: Doreen & Granville Shaw
122 High Street
Broadway
Worcestershire WR12 7AJ, England
Tel & fax: (01386) 853432
E-mail: milestone.house@talk21.com
www.karenbrown.com/england/milestonehouse.html
4 rooms
£25–£27.50 per person
Open all year
Credit cards: MC, VS
Children over 15
No-smoking house

The Buck Inn is a traditional Georgian coaching inn standing beneath the towering craggy heights of Buckden Pike which rises steeply behind it. Conviviality and good cheer are the order of the day in the bar where real ale is hand-pulled from the cool stone cellars. In summer there is always a crowd and overnight guests may prefer the quieter restaurant in a bright, enclosed courtyard where in days of old sheep auctions were held. You can enjoy a set four-course dinner with lots of choices for each course or order from the extensive bar menu. Bedrooms are country-style in their decor, the largest being a suite and four-poster room with a high, raftered ceiling. I particularly like those at the front with their view across the village to the dale. The surrounding rugged countryside offers many paths for walkers whether they prefer long day hikes or shorter strolls. Wharfedale has several lovely mellow-stone villages such as Grassington, Appletreewick, and Kettlewell. It is a spectacular drive from here through Coverdale to Middleham with its ruined castle and on to Jervaulx with its romantic ruined abbey. To the west, moorland roads lead to Arncliffe and Littondale and on to Malham (in Airedale), famous for its massive crags, tarn, and cove. *Directions:* Buckden is 18 miles north of Skipton on the B6160.

THE BUCK INN
Owners: Marjorie & Roy Hayton
Buckden
Skipton
North Yorkshire, BD23 5JA, England
Tel: (01756) 760228, Fax: (01756) 760227
E-mail: thebuckinn@yorks.net
14 rooms
£36 per person, dinner £14
Open all year
Credit cards: MC, VS
Children welcome

The clomp of hooves as horses pulled carriages down the main street of B disappeared, but the inns that provided lodging and food to weary travelers you are in search of a simple, quaint hostelry, you can do no better than to ba at The Lamb for the duration of your stay in the Cotswolds. The public are "decorated" but furnished as they have been for centuries with family antiques. rooms opening one onto another have thick stone walls, old tile floors richly worn wi patina of age, and low, beamed ceilings that have captured the wonderful aroma centuries of wood-burning fires. A tall, upholstered settle sits before the fireplace on the flagstone floor of the main room and the hall table displays gleaming brass jelly molds. An air of times long past pervades the place, particularly in winter when the air is heavy with the scent of wood smoke and a flickering fire burns in the grate. Narrow staircases and corridors zigzag up and down to the little bedrooms, all delightfully decorated in a charming cottagey style. In the dining room you make your choices from a three-course dinner menu. The homely little bar with its stone-flagged floor and wooden settles has an indefinable mixture of character and atmosphere. Burford's main street is bordered by numerous antique, gift, and tea shops. *Directions:* Burford is midway between Oxford and Cheltenham (A40). The Lamb Inn is on Sheep Street, just off the village center.

THE LAMB INN
Owners: Caroline & Richard De Wolf
Sheep Street
Burford
Oxfordshire OX18 4LR, England
Tel: (01993) 840155, Fax: (01993) 822228
15 rooms
£50–£60 per person, dinner £25
Closed Christmas, Credit cards: MC, VS
Children welcome

Map: 3d

...urford has long
...emain and if
...e yourself
...s aren't
Cozy
...h a

...eorgian townhouses fronting a broad square, Twelve Angel
... bed and breakfast operated with great professionalism by
... Clarke. Breakfast is the only meal served in the formal
...es are topped with crisp linen cloths and surrounded by
...ening guests often gather in the bar-cum-sitting room to
...y restaurants or pubs they are going to dine. Upstairs, the
...o snug and all but the four-poster room and the suite are
...y enjoyed the two large front bedrooms with spacious seating
...-poster room overlooks the back of the house). Light sleepers be aware
...ere may be a little late-night noise from the square on Fridays and Saturdays. On the
square you have the 16th-century cathedral and the church of St. Mary's (even older than
the cathedral), and nearby two museums. If you are there on a Wednesday or Saturday,
do not miss the street market. Bury St. Edmunds is an excellent center for touring East
Anglia and Lavenham and Cambridge are popular places to visit. *Directions:* Follow the
A14 to the Bury St. Edmunds ring road. Take the second exit (Bury St. Edmunds central)
then at the next roundabout turn into Northgate Street. At the T-junction turn right into
the square: Twelve Angel Hill is on your right (park at rear).

TWELVE ANGEL HILL
Owners: Bernadette (Bernie) & John Clarke
12 Angel Hill
Bury St. Edmunds
Suffolk IP33 1UZ, England
Tel: (01284) 704088, Fax: (01284) 725549
www.karenbrown.com/england/twelveangelhill.html
6 rooms
£40–£50 per person
Closed Jan
Credit cards: all major
Children over 16
No-smoking house

Built over a century ago, Chilvester Hill House is a solidly constructed Victorian home isolated from the busy A4 by a large garden. Gill and John Dilley retired here and subsequently unretired themselves: John, a physician, now works as an occupational health consultant and Gill entertains guests and breeds beef cattle. Gill enjoys cooking and a typical (optional) dinner might consist of smoked trout, lamb noisettes with vegetables from the garden, fruit fool, and cheese and biscuits. They have a short wine list with over 20 French and German wines. A soft pastel decor, treasured antiques, and a cleverly displayed collection of commemorative plates make the large, high-ceilinged drawing room the most elegant room in the house. The bedrooms are spacious, high-ceilinged rooms, each individually decorated with flowery wallpaper and two have zip-link beds that can be either a king or twins. All have mineral water, tea and coffee tray, television, tourist information, and private bathroom. Visitors can take advantage of Gill and John's maps marked with scenic routes to nearby Castle Combe, Lacock, and the Avebury Neolithic Circle. Bath, Oxford, and Salisbury are an easy drive away. *Directions:* From London leave the M4 at junction 14 and follow signs for Hungerford. Turn right on the A4 through Marlborough to Calne. Follow Chippenham signs for half a mile, turn right (Bremhill), and immediately right into the drive.

CHILVESTER HILL HOUSE
Owners: Gill & John Dilley
Calne
Wiltshire SN11 0LP, England
Tel: (01249) 813981, Fax: (01249) 814217
3 rooms
£35–£42.50 per person, dinner £18–£20
Open all year
Credit cards: all major
Children over 12
Wolsey Lodge

Magnolia House, a sturdy Georgian home converted into the most welcoming of guest houses by Ann and John Davies, sits on a quiet street just a five-minute walk from the heart of Canterbury. Ann and John offer a sincerely warm welcome to their home and mark up maps of the city so that guests can easily find their way around. A small parlor is stacked with information not only on Canterbury but the surrounding area–you can easily keep busy for a week. Delightful guestrooms are found upstairs in the house ranging in size from a snug single to lovely double-bedded room, but the gem is the Garden Room with its private garden entrance, four-poster queen-sized bed, and the most spacious of bathrooms. In summer breakfast is the only meal served but on gloomy winter evenings Ann realizes that very often guests do not want to venture out and is happy, with prior arrangement, to provide supper. Canterbury is a lively historical city easily explored on foot. Its primary attraction is its cathedral, the Mother Church for all Anglicans. Begun in 1070, it has survived fires, wars, desecration, and bombing and became a pilgrimage site after the murder of Thomas à Becket. Join Chaucer's famous pilgrims in a 20th-century re-enactment of the *Canterbury Tales* at the Canterbury Tales Museum in St. Margaret's Street. *Directions:* Arriving in Canterbury on the A2, at the first roundabout turn left for the university. St. Dunstan's Terrace is the third street on the right and Magnolia House is the first house on the left.

MAGNOLIA HOUSE
Owners: Ann & John Davies
36 St. Dunstan's Terrace
Canterbury CT2 8AX, England
Tel & fax: (01227) 765121
E-mail: magnolia_house_canterbury@yahoo.com
www.karenbrown.com/england/magnolia.html
7 rooms
£36–£55 per person, dinner (Nov to Feb) from £18
Open all year, Credit cards: all major
Children over 12, No-smoking house

Because of its quiet country location just 3 miles off the motorway, almost equidistant between Edinburgh and London, New Capernwray Farm is an ideal place to break a long, tiring journey. However, many weary travelers return for a proper country getaway to explore this unspoiled area. There really is nothing "new" about this solid, whitewashed stone farmhouse, for, despite its name, it is over 300 years old. It was bought in 1974 by Sally and Peter Townend, who supervised its complete refurbishment while preserving its lovely old features, and now offer a very warm welcome to their guests. Before dinner you enjoy an aperitif in the cozy sitting room in front of a cheerful fire and then proceed to the dining room for a candlelit dinner. Bedrooms are particularly light, bright, and cheerful in their decor. The largest bedroom, with king bed, spans the breadth of the house, has a bathroom tucked neatly under the eaves and, as in all the rooms, is well equipped with tea, coffee, biscuits, television, hairdryer, mints, and a substantial sewing kit. A twin-bedded room has an en-suite shower room and the queen-bedded room has its shower room nearby. Sally and Peter have a wealth of books and maps on the Lake District and the Yorkshire dales. *Directions:* Leave the M6 at junction 35 and from the roundabout follow signs for Over Kellet. Turn left at the T-junction into Over Kellet, then turn left at the village green: after 2 miles the farm is on the left.

NEW CAPERNWRAY FARM
Owners: Sally & Peter Townend
Capernwray, Carnforth
Lancashire LA6 1AD, England
Tel & fax: (01524) 734284
E-mail: newcapfarm@aol.com
www.karenbrown.com/england/newcapernwrayfarm.html
3 rooms, 2 en suite
£30–£35 per person, dinner £22.50
Open Mar to Oct, Credit cards: MC, VS
Children over 10, No-smoking house
Wolsey Lodge

Carlisle makes an excellent place to break the journey when traveling by car between England and Scotland. Your host, Philip Parker, an ardent enthusiast of Carlisle and the surrounding area, encourages guests to use Number Thirty One as a base for visiting the city and exploring the northern Lake District and Hadrian's Wall. One of Philip's great passions is cooking and the dinner he prepares for guests depends on what is fresh in the market that day. Philip and Judith often join guests for a chat after dinner. Upstairs, the three bedrooms are equipped to a very high standard, with TV, trouser press, tea tray, and hair dryer, and furnished in a style complementing this large Victorian terrace home. I admired the spaciousness of the Blue Room with its sparkling Mediterranean bathroom and king-sized bed and enjoyed the sunny decor of the smaller Green Room with its large dragon stenciled on the bedhead. The equally attractive Yellow Room has a half-tester bed that can be king-sized or twin and faces the front of the house. A ten-minute stroll finds you in the heart of Carlisle with its majestic cathedral and grand castle. Tullie House, an innovative museum, portrays Carlisle's place in the turbulent history of the Borders. *Directions:* Leave the M6 at junction 43 and follow Carlisle City Centre signs through five sets of traffic lights. Howard Place is the third turning on the right (before you reach the one-way system). Number 31 is at the end of the street on the left.

NUMBER THIRTY ONE
Owners: Judith & Philip Parker
31 Howard Place
Carlisle
Cumbria CA1 1HR, England
Tel & fax: (01228) 597080
E-mail: bestpep@aol.com
www.karenbrown.com/england/numberthirtyone.html
3 rooms
£34.50–£45 per person, dinner from £20
Open Mar to Nov, Credit cards: all major
Children over 16, No-smoking house

Theresa White, who hails from Edinburgh, prides herself on offering a warm Scottish welcome to her up-market bed-and-breakfast hotel located a brisk 20-minute walk from the heart of medieval Chester. When she bought Redland in the 1980s, it was very different from the flower-decked, frothily Victorian establishment you find today. Theresa has kept all the lovely woodwork and ornate plasterwork, adding modern bathrooms, central heating, vast quantities of sturdy Victorian furniture, four suits of armor, and masses of Victorian bric-a-brac. Guests help themselves to drinks at the honesty bar and relax in the sumptuous drawing room, which includes among its array of furniture high-backed armchairs that almost surround you. Traditional Scottish porridge is a must when you order breakfast in the dining room where little tables are covered with starched Victorian tablecloths. For dinner Theresa is happy to advise on where to eat in town. Pay the few extra pounds and request one of the "best" rooms, for not only are they more spacious, but you will be treated to a lovely old bed (with modern mattress, of course) and decor where everything from the draperies to the china is color-coordinated. Walking round Chester's Roman walls is a good way to orient yourself to the city. It is fun to browse in The Rows, double-decker layers of shops. *Directions:* Redland Hotel is located on the A5104, 1 mile from the city center.

REDLAND HOTEL
Owner: Theresa White
64 Hough Green
Chester CH4 8JY, England
Tel: (01244) 671024, Fax: (01244) 681309
www.karenbrown.com/england/redlandhotel.html
12 rooms
£32.50–£37.50 per person
Open all year
Credit cards: none
Children over 2

Bed & Breakfast Descriptions

Chiddingfold, with its attractive homes set round the village green, is one of the most picturesque villages on the wooded Surrey Downs. A dovecote fronts the country lane just off the village green and a path leads beside it through a picture-book English cottage garden to Greenaway, the charming home of Sheila and John Marsh. The interior is just as delightful as the exterior, with low-ceilinged, beamed rooms, each decorated to perfection without making them stiffly formal or contrived. Guests enjoy the lovely living room with its views of the garden and part of Sheila and John's collection of colorful Staffordshire pottery displayed on the mantelshelf above the massive inglenook fireplace. Breakfast is served in the cozy, antique-filled dining room. For dinner guests often walk down to one of the pubs on the village green. All bedrooms are in the original 17th-century, heavily beamed section of the house. The large front bedroom enjoys an old-fashioned bathroom with a claw-foot tub. The spacious French twin and a third small bedroom share a large, immaculate bathroom. Chiddingfold is conveniently located 40 miles from both Gatwick and Heathrow airports and London is less than an hour away by train. Guests often visit Petworth House, Bignor Roman villa, the Royal Horticultural Society gardens, Chichester, Portsmouth, and the south coast. *Directions:* From Guildford take the A3 and the A283 to Chiddingfold. Pickhurst Road is off the green and Greenaway is the third house on the left with the large dovecote in front.

GREENAWAY
Owners: Sheila & John Marsh
Pickhurst Road, Chiddingfold
Surrey GU8 4TS, England
Tel: (01428) 682920, Fax: (01428) 685078
E-mail: jfvmarsh@nildram.co.uk
www.karenbrown.com/england/greenaway.html
3 rooms, 1 en suite
£35–£40 per person
Open all year, Credit cards: MC, VS
Children welcome, No-smoking house

Ashen Clough, Isobel and Norman Salisbury's home, be
prosperous yeoman's home set in a rural Derbyshire val
the local vet then retired to take on domestic duties, help
as the most welcoming of Wolsey Lodges. Except on
hosts around the ancient refectory table in the low-bea
comfortable drawing room precede dinner and it is he
evening-long conversation before retiring to their deli
lead to main roads that quickly transport you to Georgia
house, Bakewell with its shops and Monday market, the
Royal Crown Derby factories and factory shops, and the great houses of Chatsworth,
Haddon, Keddleston, and Lyme Hall. *Directions:* From Buxton take the A6 (Manchester
road) for 6 miles and at the roundabout turn left at the signpost for Chinley. Follow the
B6062 into the village where you turn right and then right again into Maynestone Road.
Ashen Clough is on your left after 1¼ miles.

ASHEN CLOUGH
Owners: Isobel & Norman Salisbury
Maynestone Road
Chinley, High Peak
Derbyshire SK23 6AH, England
Tel: (01663) 750311, Fax: none
3 rooms, 2 en suite
£32.50–£35 per person, dinner £20
Closed occasionally
Credit cards: none
Children over 12
Wolsey Lodge

of flint-walled, tile-roofed cottages is no longer "next the sea," but it by a vast saltwater marsh formed as the sea retreated. The massive Cley Mill stands as a handsome monument to man's ability to harness the nature. Guests enter the mill directly into the beamed dining room decorated country-style pine furniture. The circular sitting room has large chintz chairs drawn a stone fireplace whose mantel is a sturdy beam displaying toby jugs. Stacked above the sitting room are two large circular bedrooms with en-suite bathrooms: the Wheat Chamber is where the grain was stored and the Stone Room is where the massive grinding stones crushed the flour. Two additional small bedrooms share a bathroom. During the day the mill is open to the public to visit the observation room and the wooden cap of the mill with its massive gears and complex mechanisms which once turned the grinding stones. The old boat house and stables in the yard have been converted into small, self-catering cottages. Birdwatching, sailing, cycling, and walking are popular pastimes in the area. The seaside towns of Sheringham, Cromer, and Wells are close at hand. There are a great many stately homes to explore such as Sandringham House, the Royal Family's country residence, Jacobean Fellbrigg Hall, Holkham, and Blickling Hall. *Directions:* From King's Lynn follow the A149 around the coast to Cley next the Sea, where the windmill is well signposted.

CLEY MILL GUEST HOUSE
Manager: Jeremy Bolan
Cley next the Sea, Holt
Norfolk NR25 7RP, England
Tel & fax: (01263) 740209
www.karenbrown.com/england/cleymillguesthouse.html
8 rooms, 6 en suite
£27.50–£44 per person, dinner £16.50
Open all year
Credit cards: MC, VS
Children welcome

Manor Farm is a peaceful haven just inland from the sea, a glorious spot to enjoy once you have overcome the challenges of finding it. This part-whitewashed stone and slate manor is a splendid old building set in acres of glorious gardens. Muriel and Paul Knight operate on house party lines, with guests gathering for drinks and introductions before dinner at 7. The dinner party is an opportunity to meet people in a convivial manner and to enjoy a sociable evening in a very English setting. The antique furnishings, paintings, and decor reflect the age and ambiance of this Domesday-listed manor. Up one staircase are two lovely little cottagey rooms while up another are three equally delightful rooms. The scenery in this part of Cornwall is stunning and best enjoyed from the coastal path that meanders up and down the clifftops. Four miles away lies the strikingly picturesque harbor of Boscastle and just beyond it Tintagel with its legends of King Arthur. *Directions:* Ten miles south of Bude on the A39 turn right for Crackington Haven. At the sea front follow the same road up the other side of the valley and turn left into a narrow lane (Church Park Road) just before the red telephone box. Take the first right (Tinier lane) and Manor Farm is in front of you after 300 yards.

MANOR FARM
Owners: Muriel & Paul Knight
Higher Crackington
Crackington Haven Nr Bude
Cornwall EX23 0JW, England
Tel: (01840) 230304, Fax: none
www.karenbrown.com/england/manorfarm.html
5 rooms
£30–£35 per person, dinner £16*
*Not available in August
Open all year
Credit cards: none
No children
No-smoking house

Nancemellan is a beautiful arts and crafts home overlooking the rugged little bay of Crackington Haven, built in 1905 for a wealthy Londoner. Lorraine and Eddie have taken great pains to keep all the lovely old features of the house with its tiled entryway, beams, and ornate door and window moldings. Guests have a lovely drawing room where a log fire is lit on chilly evenings. Breakfast is the only meal served round the large pine table in the family kitchen. Lorraine chats to guests about where to go and what to see as she cooks on the Aga. For dinner, guests can go just down the road to the pub or Lorraine is happy to make dining arrangements at local farmhouses that specialize in offering dinner for visitors. A large double bedroom offers the most glorious of sea views and has its spacious bathroom, resplendent with claw-foot tub, just across the hall. The other double-bedded room has its bathroom (also with claw-foot tub) en suite while the twin-bedded room has an adjacent bathroom. Nine acres of gardens are yours to explore. The stunning views from the house tempt you out to the coastal path, which offers the most magnificent of vistas of this rocky part of Cornwall. To the north lies Clovelly while to the south you find Boscastle and Tintagel. *Directions:* Ten miles south of Bude on the A39 turn right for Crackington Haven. As the lane begins to drop steeply towards the sea, Nancemellan is on your right.

NANCEMELLAN
Owners: Lorraine & Eddie Ruff
Crackington Haven, nr Bude
Cornwall EX23 0NN, England
Tel & fax: (01840) 230283
www.karenbrown.com/england/nancemellan.html
3 rooms, 1 en suite
£22–£28 per person
Open Easter to Oct
Credit cards: none
Children over 12
No-smoking house

Just steps from the clifftops on a secluded stretch of Cornish coast, this 16th-century farmhouse snuggles in a hollow round a cobbled courtyard. The polished flagstone floors lead you into the comfortable sitting room with high-backed sofas grouped round the log-burning stove. Guests dine at separate tables and Janet Crocker offers a hearty dinner with a choice of starter, main course, and dessert. Farmhouse bedrooms range from small to spacious. It's very much a family operation where Janet and her daughter Gayle run the farmhouse while her husband, four sons, and their wives manage the farm, tea room, and self-catering cottages. The farm is now licensed for civil marriages, offering a romantic spot to "tie the knot." The clifftops provide magnificent views and a path leads to Strangles Beach where Thomas Hardy loved to walk with his first wife Emma. Walking the coastal path and the nearby villages of Boscastle and Tintagel are great attractions. *Directions:* From Bude, take the A39 towards Camelford and then turn right to Crackington Haven. At the beach, take the right-hand turn at the bottom of the hill for Trevigue and you find Trevigue Farm atop the cliffs after 2 miles.

TREVIGUE FARM
Owners: Janet, Gayle & Ken Crocker
Trevigue, nr Crackington Haven
Bude
Cornwall EX23 0LQ, England
Tel & fax: (01840) 230418
www.karenbrown.com/england/treviguefarm.html
3 rooms
£30–£34 per person, dinner £18
Closed Christmas
Credit cards: none
Children over 12
No-smoking house

Folly Hill Cottage began life in the 1850s as a tiny farm cottage for workers on the nearby estate. Over the last 50 years every owner has added to the house and Sonia and John de Carle have done their bit with the addition of modern plumbing and more bathrooms. Guests enjoy breakfast in the snug dining room and, with advance notice, Sonia is happy to prepare a simple supper or more elaborate dinner on the night of your arrival (bring your own wine). Upstairs, a sitting nook provides a television, small refrigerator, books, and masses of information on the local area. A spacious twin-bedded room has a large bathroom and an alcove where you can prepare coffee and tea. The smaller bedroom has its private bathroom across the hall. After a day of sightseeing enjoy a refreshing swim in the pool. The garden runs down to the river, which flows either side of the main lawn, formerly the tennis court for the "big house" up the road. Sissinghurst Castle with its lovely garden is nearby and guests often visit Canterbury and its famous cathedral, which is especially impressive during choral evensong. Leeds Castle, local vineyards, and the old railway at Tenterden are other popular attractions. *Directions:* Take the A21 south from Sevenoaks to the A262 signposted Goudhurst and Cranbrook. Pass the Kennel Holt Hotel on the right and a signpost for Colliers Green on the left. After 400 yards, turn left into Friezley Lane (between white posts). Go to the very end, up a small hill, and Folly Hill Cottage is the last house but one.

FOLLY HILL COTTAGE
Owners: Sonia & John de Carle
Friezley Lane, Hocker Edge, Cranbrook
Kent TN17 2LL, England
Tel & fax: (01580) 714299
E-mail: decarlej@aol.com
2 rooms, 1 en suite
£20–£23 per person, dinner £12.50–£17.50
Closed Christmas, Credit cards: none
Children over 10
No-smoking house

Everything about The Old Cloth Hall is exceptional, from the vast expanses of gardens with manicured lawns, roses, rhododendrons, and azaleas to the dignified old house, parts of which date back more than 500 years. Settle into the richly paneled drawing room with its commodious sofas and chairs drawn round the crackling log fire which blazes in the enormous inglenook. The Old Cloth Hall has been Katherine Morgan's home for many years and because it is a large house, she has an array of bedrooms that can be used for guest accommodation, which she prices by size and location. If you want to splurge, ask for The Four-Poster room and you will receive a king-size four-poster decked and draped in lemon-and-green-sprigged fabric with an enormous bathroom. The small downstairs twin is reserved for children. Elizabeth I came for lunch in 1573 but you can stay for dinner and dine with your fellow guests. Guests are welcome to use the swimming pool and the tennis court. Sissinghurst Gardens are a mile away, while Sir Winston Churchill's home, Chartwell, Knole, Igtham Mote, Penshurt Place, and Batemans, Rudyard Kipling's home, are within easy reach. *Directions:* Take the A21 south from Sevenoaks, turn left at the A262 before Lamberhurst and right onto the A229. Go into Cranbrook and take a sharp left after the school. Follow this road for about a mile, bearing left when it forks, turn right just before the cemetery, and the entrance to The Old Cloth Hall is on your right.

THE OLD CLOTH HALL
Owner: Katherine Morgan
Cranbrook
Kent TN17 3NR, England
Tel & fax: (01580) 712220
www.karenbrown.com/england/theoldclothhall.html
3 rooms
£45–£50 per person, dinner £21
Closed Christmas, Credit cards: none
Children by arrangement
Wolsey Lodge

This quiet rural spot is just minutes from Scotch Corner on the A1, making it an ideal place to break your journey between the south of England and Scotland. David's family has always farmed in Yorkshire, and when he inherited this small farm, he moved here with Heather and built Clow Beck House. Heather and David are relaxed, welcoming people who truly enjoy sharing their home with visitors. Guests have a large formal drawing room but more often gravitate into the large country kitchen and the spacious beamed dining room with its cheery fire. After a day of sightseeing it's nice to stay home for dinner then stroll into the village for a drink. A couple of guestrooms are in the main house with the remainder occupying a stable, a granary, and cottage. (One room in the granary wing is equipped for the handicapped.) All the rooms are excellently fitted with TV, phone, bathrobes, and large umbrellas. Use this welcoming, off-the-beaten-tourist-path spot as a base for explorations to the Yorkshire Dales, Moors, and heritage coast with Whitby, Robin Hood's Bay, and Runswick. Heather and David love planning routes for guests. *Directions:* From Scotch Corner go north on the A1 for a short distance to the Barton exit. Go through Barton and Newton Morell, turn right for Croft, and after 2½ miles turn left into the farm.

CLOW BECK HOUSE
Owners: Heather & David Armstrong
Monk End Farm
Croft on Tees, Darlington
North Yorkshire DL2 2SW, England
Tel: (01325) 721075, Fax: (01325) 720419
E-mail: clow.beck.house@dial.pipex.com
www.karenbrown.com/england/clowbeckhouse.html
14 rooms
£30 per person, dinner £9–£20
Open all year
Credit cards: all major
Children welcome

The Coach House is made up of a group of several old buildings, including a 1680s cottage and an old smithy, that form a square round a courtyard fronting directly on the A697 Coldstream to Morpeth road. The cottage serves as the dining room with two rooms either side of the entrance hall. Several of the nine bedrooms open directly onto the graveled courtyard—these are equipped for wheelchair access and each has a large open-plan bathroom. Most of the guestrooms have refrigerators and all have tea- and coffee-making facilities. A decadent afternoon tea of cakes and scones is laid in the high-beamed sitting room where French doors open onto the paved patio. Lynne offers an evening meal with a set main course and lots of choices of starters and dessert including several homemade ice creams. The decor is not perfect—a tad run-down in parts—but Lynn has made inroads into redecorating and there's a lot of warmth and atmosphere to the place. Crookham makes an ideal place to break the journey between Scotland and York, but several days spent here will allow you to explore the plethora of Northumbrian castles and battlefields (Flodden is just down the road) and the delightful Northumbrian coastline between Lindisfarne (Holy Island) and the ancient port of Seahouses. *Directions:* From the south take the A1 to Morpeth and the A697 (Coldstream road) for 35 miles to Crookham where you find The Coach House on the left about a mile after the right-hand turn for Ford and Etal.

THE COACH HOUSE
Owner: Lynne Anderson
Crookham, Cornhill on Tweed
Northumberland TD12 4TD, England
Tel: (01890) 820293, Fax: (01890) 820284
www.karenbrown.com/england/thecoachhouse.html
9 rooms, 7 en suite
£23–£36 per person, dinner £16.50
Open Easter to Oct
Credit cards: MC, VS (4% extra)
Children welcome

When you stay at The Old Manor, you get far more than bed and breakfast in a 16th-century house—you can tour its motor museum, make friends with the army of ducks and geese that wander around the yard, and visit the contented, muddy pigs who wallow at the bottom of the lawn. Liz loves her beautifully manicured garden that stretches down to the edge of the Oxford Canal (you can walk for miles along its towpath)—benches tempt guests to settle and watch the flow of barge traffic. Inside, there are cozy beamed rooms and the gentle ticking of Liz and John's clock collection. Books line the walls of the breakfast room and guests eat together round the trestle table before a log fire. The small yellow sitting room at the top of the stairs is for guests to use. A large double bedroom has a snug, en-suite shower room while the two twin rooms share a bathroom down the hallway. Liz is very aware that guests always enjoy their own bathroom facilities, so she rents only one of the twin bedrooms at a time. John is happy to show you his transportation collection, which includes an AC Cobra, a 1910 AC Sociable, and a 1934 Aston Martin. If you are planning on staying for a week, consider renting the delightful little Dovehouse Barn. Warwick Castle, Coventry, and a multitude of Cotswold villages are within half an hour's drive. *Directions:* Exit the M40 at junction 11 (Banbury) and take the A361 towards Daventry for 2½ miles, turn left to Cropredy, cross the canal, turn left at the T-junction, and The Old Manor is on your left.

THE OLD MANOR
Owners: Liz & John Atkins
Cropredy, Banbury
Oxfordshire OX17 1PS, England
Tel: (01295) 750235, Fax: (01295) 758479
E-mail: old_manor@cropredy12.freeserve.co.uk
www.karenbrown.com/england/theoldmanor.html
3 rooms, 1 en suite
£25–£27.50 per person
Closed Christmas & New Year, Credit cards: MC, VS
Children welcome, No-smoking house

Delbury Hall, built in 1753, is one of the most beautiful Georgian houses in Shropshire, a grand red-brick edifice reflected in a lake with elegant swans. Despite its gracious architecture and lovely antiques, this is not an intimidating or overly grand house, but very much a home for Lucinda and Patrick Wrigley and their two young children. You enter directly into the imposing two-story entry hall with its staircase sweeping up to the gallery above. Here you find a four-poster room with a large en-suite bathroom and a suite of rooms with two bedrooms and a bathroom, which is often used for families. A spacious twin-bedded room has its private bathroom up a further flight of stairs. Guests help themselves to drinks at the honesty bar while Patrick prepares an elegant dinner with fruits and vegetables fresh from the garden. The lake includes a trout fishery where guests can try their hand at catching rainbow trout. Medieval Ludlow with its spectacular ruined castle and plethora of interesting antique shops is a ten-minute drive away. Other attractions include the Ironbridge Gorge museums and the Severn Valley Steam Railway. *Directions:* From Ludlow take the A49 north towards Shrewsbury and take the first right (B4365) signed Much Wenlock for 5 miles. Turn right on the B4368 to Diddlebury then right before the village at The Lodge for Delbury Hall. If you miss this turn, go into the village and follow signs for Delbury Trout Fishery.

DELBURY HALL
Owners: Patrick & Lucinda Wrigley
Diddlebury, nr Craven Arms
Shropshire SY7 9DH, England
Tel: (01584) 841267, Fax: (01584) 841441
E-mail: wrigley@delbury.demon.co.uk
www.karenbrown.com/england/delbury.html
4 rooms, 1 en suite
£45–£50, dinner £29
Closed Christmas
Credit cards: MC, VS
Children welcome

Hunts Tor offers the opportunity not only for very comfortable bed and breakfast accommodation but also for enjoying excellent food (Paul Henderson of Gidleigh Park assured me that, next to Gidleigh Park, Sue Harrison offers the finest food on Dartmoor). Every evening Sue prepares a set, four-course dinner and while she is busy in the kitchen husband Chris helps guests choose wine and serves at table. In 1997 Hunts Tor was nominated by the *Good Food Guide* as the "Best Small Devon Restaurant of the Year." Fortunately for diners, the Harrisons also offer the highest quality accommodation (Gidleigh Park excluded, of course!) in the area. The three very spacious bedrooms are large enough to accommodate seating areas. The raw beauty of Dartmoor with its sheltered villages and market towns, wild ponies, and spectacular scenery is a magnet for walkers and those touring by car. Just beyond the village you find Castle Drogo, the castle-like house designed by Lutyens. *Directions:* Take the M5 to Exeter and the A30 towards Okehampton for about 14 miles. Turn left for Drewsteignton (3 miles) and upon reaching the village square turn right. Hunts Tor is at the opposite end of the square from the church.

HUNTS TOR
Owners: Sue & Chris Harrison
Drewsteignton
Devon EX6 6QW, England
Tel & fax: (01647) 281228
www.karenbrown.com/england/huntstor.html
3 rooms
£30–£35 per person, dinner £20–£23
Open Mar to Oct
Credit cards: none
Children over 10

Dunster, with its adorable main street dominated by the battlements and towers of Dunster Castle, is a picture-postcard village. Dollons House, once a pharmacy whose chemist also made marmalade for the Houses of Parliament, is a gift shop of English crafts and silk flowers where proprietor Humphrey Bradshaw makes his marmalade for his family and bed and breakfast guests. Up the narrow cottage stairs guests have a cozy sitting room which leads to a patio and pocket-sized garden. Hannah Bradshaw has taken a great deal of care decorating her very pretty bedrooms. Teddy, as the name implies, has cute bears embroidered on its towels and pillows and a whimsical honey-bear mural decorating the tiny shower room. Tulips is soft and country in pale pinks with hand-painted tulips on the fabric border which edges the room. Kate's at the back of the house is delightfully white and frilly with a large bathroom and shower. Dunster Castle is open to the public and you can tour the 18th-century Dunster watermill. *Directions:* From Bridgwater take the A39 almost to Minehead. Turn left on the A396 into Dunster, and Dollons is in Church Street on your right. Pull up outside to unload then park in the High Street or behind the church.

DOLLONS HOUSE
Owners: Hannah & Humphrey Bradshaw
Church Street
Dunster
Minehead
Somerset TA24 6SH, England
www.karenbrown.com/england/dollonshouse.html
Tel: (01643) 821880, Fax: (01643) 822016
e-mail: hannah.bradshaw@virgin.net
3 rooms
£27.50–£30 per person
Closed Christmas, Credit cards: MC, VS
Children over 15, No-smoking house

Drakestone House is an exceptional Cotswold-style home filled with an abundance of lovely antiques. The well-kept grounds invite a leisurely stroll between the tall, clipped hedges laid out by Hugh's grandfather. The interior of Drakestone House has lovely old pine and jarrah wood floors and beamed and plasterwork ceilings, complemented by traditional firebaskets filled with dried-flower arrangements and beautiful old furniture. Guests enjoy breakfast round the dining-room table where Crystal will, with advance arrangements, also serve dinner for guests' first evening's stay. Upstairs, two bedrooms share the facilities of an old-fashioned bathroom, which has been modernized. There is also a suite with an adjoining private bathroom, a small single room suitable for children (crib available), and/or a larger, twin-bedded room which has windows with views both to the side and the front of the house. From Drakestone House you can visit Berkeley Castle and the adjacent Jenner Museum, Slimbridge Wildfowl Trust, Westonbirt Arboretum, and, farther afield, Gloucester, Cheltenham, Bath, and Bristol. *Directions:* Northbound travelers leave the M5 at exit 14; southbound at exit 13. Stinchcombe is situated halfway between Dursley and Wotton-under-Edge on the B4060. Drakestone House is signposted on the road.

DRAKESTONE HOUSE
Owners: Crystal & Hugh St. John Mildmay
Stinchcombe
Dursley
Gloucestershire GL11 6AS, England
Tel: (01453) 542140, Fax: none
3 rooms
£28 per person, dinner £17.50
Open Mar to Nov
Credit cards: none
Children welcome
No-smoking house

Ronald's acres of garden have been voted among the top three in Somerset: plant-filled borders line the tumbling stream, the herbaceous border is ablaze with summer flowers, and the water meadow offers some unusual plant species. Jackie loves to share her beautiful home with guests who can choose from three very different bedrooms. The Cottage Suite offers a low-ceilinged bedroom, snug sitting room with television and sofas that can be made into extra beds, and a small bathroom. In contrast, the Master Suite offers a spacious high-ceilinged room with a queen-sized bed, television, and a large, luxurious Victorian-style bathroom. The Pine Bedroom takes its name from the enormous pine fitted cupboard that has been there since the house was built. For dinner try the Foresters Arms, just a two-minute walk away. There are ten classic gardens in South Somerset. Wells and Glastonbury are within easy touring distance, as is the Dorset Coast. *Directions:* From Yeovil, take the A30 (Crewkerne road) for 2 miles to the Yeovil Court Hotel. Turn immediately left at the signpost for North Coker, and Hardington. Pass the Foresters Arms, and Holywell House is the next driveway on the right. (Ignore all signposts for East Coker.)

HOLYWELL HOUSE
Owners: Jackie & Ronald Somerville
Holywell
East Coker
Yeovil
Somerset BA22 9NQ, England
Tel: (01935) 862612, Fax: (01935) 863035
E-mail: b&b@holywellhouse.freeserve.co.uk
www.karenbrown.com/england/holywellhouse.html
3 rooms
£35–£45 per person
Closed Christmas & New Year
Credit cards: none
Children welcome

Sitting in acres of glorious gardens, Old Whyly is the most gracious of 17th-century manor houses and home to Sarah Burgoyne and her sons, a home they love to share with their guests. Sarah has a gracious, easy way with her that soon has guests feeling at home. She encourages them to relax in the beautiful drawing room, sit in the garden, swim in the pool, or take a peaceful walk through adjacent farms. Guests gravitate to the long pine table in the huge farmhouse kitchen where Sarah loves to talk to them—except when she is involved in one of the more complicated dinner dishes. Cooking is a passion for Sarah and it would be a shame to stay here and not enjoy dinner with other guests at the large round dining table. Bedrooms are most attractive. Tulip offers the most spacious accommodation; French has blue toile wallpaper, drapes, and bedspread, and wisteria peeping in at the windows; Chinese has its large private bathroom across the hall. Old Whyly is perfect for opera fans as Glyndebourne is ten minutes away and hampers can be provided. Guests often visit Charleston Garden where the Bloomsbury set used to gather. Brighton is popular for its pavilion and interesting shops in the narrow lanes, while Nymans and Leonardslee are popular gardens. *Directions:* Take the A22 south from Uckfield past Halland for half a mile then take the first left off the large roundabout towards East Hoathly. After half a mile turn left into the drive by the post box. Where the drive divides into three, take the central gravel drive to Old Whyly.

OLD WHYLY
Owner: Sarah Burgoyne
East Hoathly
East Sussex BN8 6EL, England
Tel: (01825) 840216, Fax: (01825) 840738
3 rooms, 2 en suite
£45 per person, dinner £22
Open all year, Credit cards: none
Children over 10
Wolsey Lodge

When Mary and Tony Dakin bought The Old Parsonage at an auction, it was in a sad state of disrepair and they have put a great deal of work into making it the lovely home you see today. In the days when clerics were men of substance, there were six servants for thc house and garden, but now it's just Mary, Tony, their two sons, and the tractor-mower. In the morning, Tony cooks breakfast while Mary assists guests. Typical of grand Georgian houses, the rooms are tall and spacious and the Dakins have furnished them in a most delightful manner. Two of the bedrooms have double-bedded four-posters while the third is a spacious twin-bedded room. One of the four-poster rooms has a shower room while the other two rooms have bathrooms with large tubs and separate showers. Tony is a keen gardener—the sunny conservatory is always full of plants—and photographer—photos of longtime village residents line the hallway and historic Frant pictures, together with Mary's tapestries of village scenes, adorn the dining room. Frant is a most attractive village set round a green, with two pubs and a restaurant where guests usually go for dinner. Information folders in the bedrooms give details on the 15 houses, castles, and gardens to visit in the area. London is a 40-minute train ride from Frant station. *Directions:* From Tunbridge Wells, take the A267 south for 2½ miles to Frant. Turn left at the 30 mph Frant sign, and The Old Parsonage is on your left, just before the church.

THE OLD PARSONAGE
Owners: Mary & Tony Dakin
Church Lane, Frant, Tunbridge Wells
Kent TN3 9DX, England
Tel & fax: (01892) 750773
E-mail: oldparson@aol.com
www.karenbrown.com/england/theoldparsonage.html
3 rooms
£32.50–£37 per person
Open all year
Credit cards: MC, VS
Children over 7
No smoking house

The soothing sound of water splashing down the mill race is the only sound that breaks the countryside peace and quiet when you stay at Maplehurst Mill, the site of a mill since 1309. Heather feels that eating here is an integral part of the stay and guests dine by candlelight in the ancient miller's house with its beams and inglenook fireplace. Bottomend, a ground-floor bedroom, sits directly above the mill race and its windows open onto the moss-covered millwheel. Topend, at the top of the mill, has a beamed bathroom and the four-poster room, which overlooks the meadows, has its bed strategically placed on the sloping floor. The room across the garden in the stables lacks the warm country character of those in the mill. A heated swimming pool overlooks the fields. Idencroft Herb Gardens are just round the corner and Brattle Farm, an old-fashioned working farm, is an excellent choice for those who have visited all Kent's castles, gardens, and stately homes. *Directions:* From the M20 take the A229 Hastings exit and follow Hastings signs through Maidstone for 12 miles to Staplehurst. At the end of the village turn left into the Frittenden road. After 1¼ miles, opposite a white house, turn right into a narrow lane. At the end turn right and the mill is at the foot of the incline.

MAPLEHURST MILL
Owners: Heather & Kenneth Parker
Mill Lane
Frittenden
Kent TN17 2DT, England
Tel: (01580) 852203, Fax: (01580) 852117
E-mail: maplehurst@clara.net
www.karenbrown.com/england/maplehurstmill.html
5 rooms
£32–£38 per person, dinner £22
Open all year
Credit cards: MC, VS
Children over 12, No-smoking house
Wolsey Lodge

With its acres of lovely gardens, grass tennis court, and heated swimming pool, Ennys is an idyllic, 17th-century manor house set deep in the Cornish countryside, 3 miles from St. Michael's Mount. You reach it along a private lane, and I timed my arrival perfectly—the kettle had just boiled, and I settled down for afternoon tea in the spacious country-pine kitchen. Polished flagstones line the hallway leading to the comfortable sitting room with its sofas drawn round the fire and mementos of Gill's extensive travels. Breakfast is the only meal served but Gill is happy to make reservations at local inns and restaurants for dinner. Upstairs are three lovely bedrooms, two of them delectable four-posters. Families are welcome in the suites, which occupy an adjacent barn—bedrooms here are also delightfully appointed, though without the bric-a-brac that can be so hazardous to children. Gill has three architect-designed self-catering cottages for longer stays. St. Michael's Mount is a "must visit." A delightful day trip involves an hour's walk (or a short drive) to the station to take a train to St. Ives to visit the Tate Gallery, which displays the work of 20th-century St. Ives artists. *Directions:* From Exeter, take the A30 to Crowlas village (4 miles before Penzance). Turn towards Helston, at the roundabout, and at the next roundabout turn left for Relubbus. Go through Goldsithney to St. Hilary, and when the Ennys Farm's signpost is on the right, turn left and follow the lane to the farm.

ENNYS FARM
Owner: Gill Charlton
St. Hilary, Goldsithney, Penzance
Cornwall TR20 9BZ, England
Tel: (01736) 740262, Fax: (01736) 740055
E-mail: ennys@zetnet.co.uk
www.karenbrown.com/england/ennysfarm.html
5 rooms, 3 cottages
£25–£35 per person
Open mid-Feb to mid-Nov, Credit cards: MC, VS
Children over 3 welcome in family suites

Ashfield House sits on a quiet little courtyard just off Grassington's main street. I loved this 17th-century house from the moment I stepped through the low doorway into the quaint little parlor where an old polished settle sits beside a massive log-burning fireplace. Another little sitting room has groupings of chairs and an honesty bar where guests enjoy a pre-dinner drink before going into the little cottagey dining room. Keith offers a set three-course dinner with choices of starters and dessert (dinner is not served Wednesday and Saturday May to October). In the winter and spring when guests return earlier from sightseeing and walking, Linda and Keith offer scones and tea at 4:30 pm and then a three-course dinner at 7. The bedrooms open up beyond their low doors and some are quite spacious. Two have lovely views of the garden while one has a close-up view of the adjacent cottage but the advantage of a larger bathroom. All bedrooms have compact shower rooms, TVs, and tea-making facilities. To experience some magnificent scenery, take a breathtaking circular drive from Grassington and back again through Littondale, over the fells to Malham Cove, and back to the village. *Directions:* From Skipton take the B6265 to Grassington. Turn into the main street, pass the cobbled square, and turn sharp left after the Devonshire Hotel onto a cobbled access road that leads to Ashfield House.

ASHFIELD HOUSE
Owners: Linda & Keith Harrison
Grassington
Skipton
North Yorkshire BD23 5AE, England
Tel & fax: (01756) 752584
E-mail: keilin@talk21.com
7 rooms
£33–£43 per person, dinner £18
Open Feb to Christmas
Credit cards: MC, VS
Children over 5, No-smoking house

Long ago the two principal farms in this area were Great Sir Hughes and Little Sir Hughes. Great Sir Hughes was dismantled stone by stone and taken to America while "Little" went on to greater things, with a substantial new addition in the 1700s. Now the much-loved home of Glen and David Perry, Little Sir Hughes offers a spaciousness and luxury in its accommodation that is usually considered the prerogative of country house hotels. The three bedrooms are decorated in soft pastels and kitted out with every available extra so that guests feel thoroughly spoiled—chocolates on the pillow and an extensive selection of videos are the order of the day here. Glen loves cooking and bakes her own bread, and takes full advantage of all the vegetables and fruit that she grows in her large garden from which she makes preserves and chutneys. Guests dine together in the pine-paneled dining room and toast their toes in front of a log-burning fire in the luxurious drawing room on a chilly evening. From nearby Chelmsford station it is only 35 minutes on the train to London. Cambridge is an hour's drive away, Colchester, the oldest town in Essex, a half hour, while the old port of Maldon with its sailing barges is close at hand. *Directions:* Leave the M25 at exit 28 and take the A12 to Chelmsford, leaving at the A114 Chelmsford/A130 Southend exit. Take the first slip road signposted Great Baddow, turn first left on West Hanningfield Road, and after 1 mile cross the A12 and turn immediately left for Little Sir Hughes.

LITTLE SIR HUGHES
Owners: Glen & David Perry
West Hanningfield Road
Great Baddow, Chelmsford
Essex CM2 7SZ, England
Tel: (01245) 471701, Fax: (01245) 478023
E-mail: accom@englishlive.co.uk
3 rooms
£26–£35 per person, dinner £18.50
Open all year, Credit cards: none
Children over 10, No-smoking house

Sitting beside the village green at the heart of this quiet, unspoilt Cotswold village, The Lamb is a lovely hostelry. Locals gather in the evening in the quaint bar where pride of place is given to a picture gallery of guide dogs for the blind who have been sponsored by patrons' donations. Decked out in pine, the restaurant with its soft pastel colors is most attractive and cozy. The menu is à la carte, with such dishes as beef Wellington and grilled lamb cutlets with onion sauce—an understandable specialty of the house. Simpler fare is served in the bar and adjacent buttery. Up the narrow, winding staircase and down twisting, narrow corridors you find an array of cottage-style bedrooms, all furnished differently (suitable only for the nimble of foot). Two have intricately carved four-poster beds made by Richard. Thick stone walls with deeply set windows, low ceilings, quaint doors, and beams all add to the old-world feel. A separate cottage accessed off the flagstone terrace houses two recent room additions: Jemima's House and Millie's House, both popular choices, spacious and furnished with king-size beds. The two rooms in the converted stable are not as attractive. Most people come here to tour the picturesque Cotswold villages, explore gardens such as Hidcote, and visit Stratford-upon-Avon and Oxford. *Directions:* From the A429 turn into Bourton-on-the-Water, carry on along this road (not into the village), and take the first turn right to Great Rissington.

THE LAMB INN
Owners: Kate & Richard Cleverly
Great Rissington
Bourton-on-the-Water
Gloucestershire GL54 2LD, England
Tel: (01451) 820388, Fax: (01451) 820724
www.karenbrown.com/england/thelambinn.html
14 rooms
£25–£45 per person, dinner £15–£20
Closed Christmas
Credit cards: all major
Children welcome

Church House, a spacious Georgian home, has a sweep of driveway circling to the front door beneath massive copper beeches. To the rear are lawns, sheep pasture, and a helicopter landing pad for those who care to arrive by air. Guests have a high-ceilinged, comfortable yellow drawing room where Anna displays her collection of paintings by West-Country artist Reg Gammon. Anna is happy, with advance notice, to prepare dinner. Guests eat together round the long polished table and you are welcome to bring your own wines. A graceful wooden staircase spirals its way up to the top floor and the homey guestrooms. The largest bedroom has its private bathroom across the hall while the other three rooms have their facilities in the room, artfully concealed behind tall wooden screens. Ask for the one with the view from the loo of Grittleton rooftops. On the landing is an information table showing all the things to do and see in the area, though guests are welcome to spend their days relaxing around the heated swimming pool. Grittleton is well placed to visit Bath, Bristol, Malmesbury, Tetbury, and the picture-perfect village of Castle Combe. Every May the Badminton horse trials are held nearby. *Directions:* Exit the M4 at junction 17, taking the A429 towards Cirencester, and almost immediately (at the crossroads) turn left for the 3½-mile drive to Grittleton. Church House is beside the church.

CHURCH HOUSE
Owners: Anna & Michael Moore
Grittleton, Chippenham
Wiltshire SN14 6AP, England
Tel: (01249) 782562, Fax: (01249) 782546
www.karenbrown.com/england/churchhouse.html
4 rooms, 3 en suite
£29.50 per person, dinner £18.50
Open all year
Credit cards: none
Children under 2 & over 12

Surrounded by a sky-wide landscape of fields, this converted 19th-century oast offers spacious accommodation within a half hour's drive of Kent's most celebrated tourist attractions. The lower half of the roundels, where the hops were roasted, has been converted into a spacious sitting room, but, more often than not, guests gather in the open-plan kitchen, which was formerly a barn. Anne is happy to provide dinner with advance notice. Two bedrooms (a twin and a double) occupy the upper reaches of the roundels and share a well-equipped bathroom. The third bedroom is very large and has its bathroom en suite. Sasha, the friendly golden retriever, is a great favorite with guests. Anne gives her guests lists of places to visit and a map of pubs and restaurants in the area to assist them in making sightseeing and dining decisions. Nearby places of interest include Chartwell (Churchill's home), 13th-century Hever Castle, the onetime home of the Boleyn family, and Penshurst Place, a 14th-century manor house. *Directions:* From Tonbridge, take the A26 towards Maidstone. After the village of Hadlow, pass Leavers Manor Hotel on the right and turn right into Stanford Lane. Leavers Oast is the third driveway on your right.

LEAVERS OAST
Owners: Anne & Denis Turner
Stanford Lane
Hadlow
Tonbridge
Kent TN11 0JN, England
Tel & fax: (01732) 850924
E-mail: denis@leavers-oast.freeserve.co.uk
www.karenbrown.com/england/leaversoast.html
3 rooms, 1 en suite
£27.50–£31 per person, dinner £22
Open all year
Credit cards: none
Children over 12, No-smoking house

There are many good reasons to visit Leicestershire and this exceptional home at the edge of a peaceful village with many picturesque thatched cottages is one of them. Here old furniture is gleamingly polished, the windows sparkle, and everything is in apple-pie order. The evening sun streams into the drawing room where books on stately homes and castles invite browsing. Breakfast is served in a small dining room with a long trestle table. If there are several people for dinner, Raili (who grew up in Finland) sets the elegant table in the large dining room and serves a variety of meals using organic vegetables from her garden. The principal bedroom has en-suite facilities, while the other guestrooms have either private bathrooms or shower rooms. Bedrooms have televisions and someone is always on hand to make a pot of tea. A three-day Christmas program gives guests the opportunity to experience a quiet, traditional English country Christmas—visits to the hunt and the midnight carol service are highlights. Nearby are a great many stately homes (Burghley House and Rockingham Castle, for instance), lots of antique shops, cathedrals at Ely and Peterborough, historic towns (Stamford and Uppingham), and ancient villages. *Directions:* From Uppingham take the A47 and turn left at East Norton for Hallaton. Drive through the village and The Old Rectory is next to the church.

THE OLD RECTORY
Owners: Raili & Tom Fraser
Hallaton, Market Harborough
Leicestershire LE16 8TY, England
Tel: (01858) 555350, Fax: none
www.karenbrown.com/england/hallaton.html
3 rooms, 2 en suite
£32 per person, dinner £18.50
Open all year
Credit cards: none
Children over 7
No-smoking house
Wolsey Lodge

Hamsterley Forest, a vast woodland with clearings and streams nestling beneath wide expanses of moorland 40 miles south of Hadrian's Wall, is a noted beauty spot. Helene's grandparents used to love walking here and were so captivated by the tranquil setting of the grand crumbling hunting lodge they found that they moved in and set about its complete restoration. Now the house is divided into three and Helene is fortunate enough to occupy the largest section with its high-ceilinged baronial dining room. Guests gather here for a delicious dinner after enjoying canapés in the comfortable sitting room (bring your own wine). Upstairs, the large front bedroom has a huge bathroom with sunken tub, while the pink and blue rooms are small only by comparison. Should you tire of walking, Raby Castle, Bowes Museum, and Killhope Wheel (a mining museum) are all nearby. Beamish Open Air Museum, Hadrian's Wall, and Durham Cathedral make popular day trips. It's a perfect place to take a few days' break on the way to or from Scotland. *Directions:* Leave the A1 at Darlington and take the A68 towards Consett for 15 miles where you turn left at the brown signs for Hamsterley Forest (2 miles after Toft Hill). Go through Hamsterley village (ignore forest signs) and continue for 2 miles, turning right at the sign "The Grove." Follow the road left then take the next right into the forest at the Grove House signpost. After 3 miles go over a stone bridge—the house faces you.

GROVE HOUSE
Owners: Helene & Russell Close
Hamsterley Forest, Bishop Auckland
Co Durham DL13 3NL, England
Tel: (01388) 488203, Fax: (01388) 488174
E-mail: xov47@dial.pipex.com
www.karenbrown.com/england/grovehouse.html
3 rooms
£26.50–£28.50 per person, dinner £19.50
Closed mid-Dec to mid-Jan
Credit cards: none
Children over 8, No-smoking house

Surrounded by lush green fields, Greenlooms Cottage offers a quiet countryside location just 5 miles from the heart of medieval Chester. The cottage was the hedger-and-ditcher's cottage on the Duke of Westminster's Eaton estate. Hezekiah, the last incumbent, lived here for many years with his sister Miriam who raised pigs and geese. Now Greenlooms is home to Deborah and Peter Newman who have sympathetically extended and modernized the cottage, while keeping all its lovely old features such as the low, beamed ceilings and the pump in the garden. Step through the front door into the old-fashioned pine country kitchen where Deborah serves breakfast. Through the snug television room you come to the cottagey little bedrooms. For dinner, Deborah usually suggests the Grosvenor Arms in Aldford or dining in the atmospheric bar at nearby Willington Hall. Rather than looking for parking in the center of Chester, drive to the Park and Ride from where a shuttle bus transports you into town (runs every ten minutes till 6 pm). Conwy Castle and Bodnant Gardens in Wales are a very popular day trip. *Directions:* From Chester take the A41 (Whitchurch road) south for 2 miles, and turn left at Whitehouse Antiques (before the Black Dog pub). Follow the road through the village for 1½ miles, turn right into Martins Lane, and Greenlooms Cottage is on your right, after less than a mile.

GREENLOOMS COTTAGE
Owners: Deborah & Peter Newman
Hargrave
Chester
Cheshire CH3 7RY, England
Tel: (01829) 781475, Fax: none
www.karenbrown.com/england/greenlooms.html
2 rooms
£25–£30 per person, dinner £12.50
Open all year
Credit cards: none
Children welcome, No-smoking house

Built in the 14th and 15th centuries with 20th-century additions, The Hatch, painted a delectable shade of ice-cream orange, has upper-story bedroom windows peeping out from beneath a steep thatched roof. This idyllic exterior is complemented by its welcoming owners, Bridget and Robin Oaten, and the most attractive of interiors furnished with lovely antiques. Guests have a cozy, beamed sitting room with a sofa and chairs grouped round a huge fireplace. Breakfast is the only meal served in the adjacent dining room with its ancient steep staircase leading upstairs to a cottage-cozy queen bedroom and its darling en-suite bathroom. The adjacent sweet little single room is available for a child or can be used to form a suite of rooms for friends traveling together. Beyond the kitchen lies a very spacious twin-bedded room with French windows opening to a private patio overlooking the apple orchard and fields. This bedroom has the added bonus of a small kitchen, spacious, immaculate bathroom, and a private entry. Long Melford with its two stately homes and plethora of antique shops is a popular nearby town to visit, as is Lavenham with its ancient Guildhall. Bury St. Edmunds, Ely, and Cambridge are also popular destinations. *Directions:* From Bury St. Edmunds take the A143 south towards Haverhill and turn left on the B1066 signposted Glemsford. After 6 miles turn left at the cluster of cottages—The Hatch is the first house down the lane on the right. If you find yourself at the village green you have gone too far.

THE HATCH
Owners: Bridget & Robin Oaten
Pilgrims Lane
Cross Green, Hartest
Suffolk IP29 4ED, England
Tel & fax: (01284) 830226
3 rooms, 2 en suite
£25–£30 per person
Closed Christmas
Credit cards: none
Children over 9, No-smoking house

It was love at first sight when I came upon Carr Head Farm sitting high above Hathersage village with steep crags and windswept heather moors as a backdrop. The garden presents a large flagstone patio, a profusion of flowers nestled in little niches in the terraces leading down to a sweeping lawn, and the most spectacular view across this beautiful Derbyshire valley. The beauty of Mary Bailey's gardens is matched by the loveliness of her home where everything has been done with caring and impeccable taste. The beamed dining room is furnished in period style with groupings of tables and chairs where guests gather for breakfast, the only meal served. The adjacent drawing room is very elegant in blues and creams, a bowl of sweets sitting on the coffee table next to a stack of interesting books. The two lovely bedrooms have en-suite facilities. The larger bedroom offers beautiful views of the valley. The Peak District with its picturesque villages, stone-walled fields, and dramatic dales is on your doorstep, as are Haddon Hall and Chatsworth House. *Directions:* Exit the M1 at junction 29 towards Baslow where you take the A623 to the B6001, through Grindleford to Hathersage. At the junction with the main road, turn right up the village, left into School Lane, and first left. Just before the church (Little John of Robin Hood fame has his grave in the churchyard) turn right up Church Bank to the farm.

CARR HEAD FARM
Owners: Mary & Michael Bailey
Church Bank, Hathersage
Hope Valley S32 1BR, England
Tel: (01433) 650383, Fax: (01433) 651441
2 rooms
£27.50–£35 per person
Closed Christmas
Credit cards: none
Children over 12
No-smoking house

Sheltered in a gentle fold of the hills beneath the spectacular crags of Haytor Rocks, Haytor Vale is a quiet village containing little cottages and The Rock Inn. With its wooden beams and huge open fireplace, the inn has a cozy, traditional ambiance. Bedrooms are named after horses that have won the Grand National: Lovely Cottage has an old oak four-poster bed and a dark-beamed ceiling, Master Robert and Freebooter are rooms with sloping ceilings and large private bathrooms. A relatively small supplement is charged for these deluxe rooms, and it is well worth paying. All the bedrooms have television (including a movie channel), tea and coffee, telephone, and a mini bar. The food here is delightful: bar meals range from traditional roasts to curries (the desserts are especially tempting), while the candlelit restaurant serves a set-price dinner with a wide variety of choices for each course. From the giant rocky outcrop of neighboring Haytor Rocks you can see the vast extent of Dartmoor National Park, the Teign estuary, and the rolling hills of southern Devon. The nearby quarry supplied the stone used for building London Bridge, which now resides in America. *Directions:* Take the M5 from Exeter, which joins the A38, Plymouth road, then the A382 to Bovey Tracey. At the first roundabout turn left and follow the road up to Haytor and cross a cattle grid onto the moor. At the red telephone box, turn left into Haytor Vale.

THE ROCK INN
Owner: Christopher Graves
Haytor Vale
Newton Abbot
Devon TQ13 9XP, England
Tel: (01364) 661305, Fax: (01364) 661242
E-mail: rockinn@eclipse.co.uk
www.karenbrown.com/england/rockinn.html
9 rooms
£49.50–£60 per person, dinner from £25
Open all year, Credit cards: AX, VS
Children welcome

Helm is a scattering of farmhouses sitting high on the open hillside offering magnificent views of Wensleydale. On the far right of this group of houses you find the 17th-century farmhouse also called Helm—John and Barbara's home. A colony of doves in the ornamental dovecote adds to the charm of the place. A tiny entrance hall brings you into the stone-flagged dining room with its beamed ceiling (there arc over 40 choices of wine with dinner). At the bottom of the little staircase you find a massive stone cheese press which was formerly used in the farmhouse for the production of Wensleydale cheese. Two delightful bedrooms, a twin and a double, facing the front of the house have panoramic dales views and compact shower rooms. A third bedroom, a very snug and cozy double room, faces the rear of the house and has a larger bathroom with a Victorian tub. The nearby Kings Arms pub has an old-fashioned bar that appeared as the Drovers Arms in the James Herriot television series. A short walk over the fields brings you to the dramatic waterfalls of Whitfield Gill and Mill Gill. Farther afield lies the village of Hawes where you can visit the Wensleydale Creamery to watch cheese being produced. *Directions:* Take the A684 through Wensleydale to Bainbridge. Cross the river (signpost, Askrigg) and immediately after going round a sharp right-hand bend turn left (small signpost, Helm) up a narrow lane that goes up steeply into open countryside to the hamlet of Helm.

HELM COUNTRY HOUSE
Owners: Barbara & John Drew
Helm, Askrigg, near Leyburn
North Yorkshire DL8 3JF, England
Tel & fax: (01969) 650443
E-mail: holiday@helmyorkshire.com
www.karenbrown.com/england/helmcountryhouse.html
3 rooms
£30–£38 per person, dinner £18.50
Closed Nov to Jan 2
Credit cards: MC, VS
Children over 10, No-smoking house

Cobblestones border the main street of Helperby, a village where the number of shops (four) just outnumbers the pubs. Fronting onto the narrow lane that leads to the church, Brafferton Hall was built in the 1740s as the dower house to the much grander Helperby Hall. Now it is home to Sue and John White who find that their home's spacious, well-proportioned rooms are perfect for entertaining guests country-house-style. Sue and John have an easy, friendly manner, so it is a pleasure to join them in the garden for pre-dinner drinks, dine with them, and chat afterwards over coffee and chocolates. (Sue thoughtfully feeds children an early supper so that they can be tucked up in bed by dinner time.) Upstairs, the spacious Garden Room has an en-suite bathroom with claw-foot tub. T's Room offers twin beds and a shower room, while the smaller Pine Room, a double, is decked out with pine furniture and also has a shower room. Sue finds the snug double room with shower perfect for singles or older children. Brafferton Hall is ideal for exploring not only the Yorkshire dales and moors, but also Rievaulx and Fountains abbeys, Castle Howard, Whitby, and York. *Directions:* Leave the A1 at Boroughbridge and follow the Easingwold road to Helperby. Turn right at the junction and right again up Hall Lane: Brafferton Hall is on your left after 100 yards.

BRAFFERTON HALL
Owners: Sue & John White
Helperby, York
North Yorkshire Y06 2NZ, England
Tel & fax: (01423) 360352
Email: whitejohn@compuserve.com
www.karenbrown.com/england/braffertonhall.html
4 rooms
£35–£38 per person, dinner £19.50
Open all year
Credit cards: all major
Children welcome, No-smoking house
Wolsey Lodge

East Peterel Field Farm offers spectacular views of rolling countryside with hardly another building in sight, yet you are only just over a mile from the delightful market town of Hexham, and 2 miles from Hadrian's Wall, the bleak, northernmost outpost of the Roman Empire. The glory of East Peterel Field Farm is its vast country kitchen where guests enjoy breakfast at the long trestle table in front of tall windows framing idyllic countryside views. Susan loves to cook, so specials such as salmon cakes and kedgeree are often served at breakfast time (she often gives cookery demonstrations or invites guest chefs to demonstrate their arts). Guests dine together round the dining-room table and are encouraged to bring their own wine to accompany their meal. If she has a large dinner party, Susan serves coffee in the lovely drawing room, but for smaller parties she utilizes the snug, a most attractive room full of comfortable chairs where a log fire bids a cheery welcome. The master bedroom is vast, the twin room lovely, and the small double has its bathroom just next door. David runs a small stud farm where he breeds and raises thoroughbreds—his dream is to breed a Derby winner. Hadrian's Wall is a great attraction hereabouts. The beautiful Northumbrian coast with all its castles is about a 40-mile drive away. *Directions:* From Hexham, turn into Blanchland Road, at the Tap and Spile pub, bear right at the Y for 1 mile, and take the first farm track to your right after the Black House restaurant.

EAST PETEREL FIELD FARM
Owners: Susan & David Carr
Hexham, Northumberland NE46 2JT, England
Tel: (01434) 607209, Fax: (01434) 601753
E-mail: bookings@petfield.demon.co.uk
www.karenbrown.com/england/eastpeterelfieldfarm.html
3 rooms, 2 en suite
£24–£29 per person, dinner £19.50
Open all year
Credit cards: none
Children welcome, No-smoking house

This timbered pink house and its black-painted wooden barn hug a quiet country road on the edge of the peaceful Suffolk village of Higham. Meg Parker, with her gentle dalmatian Crumpet at her heels, offers a warm smile and a sincere welcome to her home, quickly putting visitors at ease. Meg leads her guests to the lovely drawing room and then escorts them up the broad staircase to their rooms. Breakfast is enjoyed around the large dining-room table and, since it is the only meal served, she is happy to offer advice on where to dine, often suggesting The Angel at Stoke by Nayland. Bedrooms vary in size from large twin-bedded rooms to a cozy double room, in the oldest part of the house, with an en-suite bathroom. Outside, Meg's large garden is carefully tended and stretches towards the River Brett where a punt and a canoe are available for guests' use. The narrow Brett soon becomes the broader Stour and you can punt/paddle upstream for a picnic and idly drift home or go downstream to Stratford St. Mary and work off a lunch at The Swan by making your way back upstream. A swimming pool is tucked into one sheltered corner of the garden and a well-kept tennis court occupies another. A highlight of a stay here is to visit Flatford, immortalized in the paintings of John Constable. *Directions:* Leave the A12 between Colchester and Ipswich at Stratford St. Mary. The Old Vicarage is 1 mile to the west next to the church.

THE OLD VICARAGE
Owner: Meg Parker
Higham, Colchester
Suffolk CO7 6JY, England
Tel: (0120) 6337248, Fax: none
www.karenbrown.com/england/theoldvicaragehigham.html
3 rooms, 1 en suite
£25–£29 per person
Open all year, Credit cards: none
Children welcome
Wolsey Lodge

Horsleygate Hall nestles in the sheltered Cordwell Valley at the edge of the Peak District National Park. The hall was built in 1783 as a farmhouse and later extended in 1836. Margaret and Robert have been careful to preserve all its old features such as the old farmhouse kitchen with its blackened Yorkshire range, flagstone floors, and the old pine woodwork and doors. Guests have a comfortable, homey sitting room and enjoy breakfast in the old schoolroom next door. Visitors often go to the Trout Inn in Barlow or the Robin Hood in Holmesfield for dinner. The attractive, spacious bedrooms enjoy views of the magnificent garden and superb Peak District scenery. The lovely garden contains many enchanting treasures: terraces, flower-filled borders, rock gardens, pools, and woodland paths. A grand garden on an infinitely larger scale surrounds Chatsworth House, the enormous home of the Duke and Duchess of Devonshire, which is full of opulent rooms and priceless paintings and furniture. Haddon Hall, a romantic, 14th-century manor house, has a fragrant rose garden. Bakewell, Ilam, Edensor, Hartington, Ashford-in-the-Water, and Eyam are particularly attractive villages in this area. *Directions:* Leave the M1 motorway at junction 29 into Chesterfield where you take the B6051 (Hathersage) through Barlow and Millthorpe, then take the first turn right (Horsleygate Lane) and immediately left into Horsleygate Hall's driveway.

HORSLEYGATE HALL
Owners: Margaret & Robert Ford
Horsleygate Lane
Holmesfield, near Chesterfield
Derbyshire S18 7WD, England
Tel: (0114) 2890333, Fax: none
3 rooms, 1 en suite
£20–£22.50 per person
Closed Christmas
Credit cards: none
Children over 5, No-smoking house

The first thing you notice when you come through Woodhayes' front door is the portraits, huge paintings that sometimes stretch from floor to ceiling. Once you have made yourself at home in this friendly house, you may be inclined, as I was, to do a "who's who" of Noel's forbears, ascertaining how the congenial pictures in your room are related to all the others. Guests dine by candlelight round the polished dining-room table in what was at one time the home's kitchen—hence the flagstone floors and huge inglenook fireplace which now contains a wood-burning stove. The twin-bedded room at the front of the house has commanding views across the valley while the four-poster room overlooks the rose garden at the side of the house. Both have en-suite bathrooms. A single bedroom has its private bathroom down the hall. Dumpdon Celtic hill fort rises behind the house and beyond lies the rolling green of the Blackdown Hills, a wonderful place for walking. Nearby Honiton is the historic center for lace making and a small museum chronicles the industry's history and development. A 20-minute drive brings you to the Victorian resort of Sidmouth and Beer, a fishing village in a little bay. *Directions:* Woodhayes is prominently visible on high ground 1½ miles northeast of Honiton. Take the Dunkeswell road, cross the River Otter, and take the first turn right. Woodhayes' drive is the first on the left.

WOODHAYES
Owners: Christy & Noel Page-Turner
Honiton
Devon EX14 0TP, England
Tel & fax: (01404) 42011
www.karenbrown.com/england/woodhayes.html
3 rooms, 2 en suite
£35 per person, dinner £22.50
Closed Feb
Credit cards: MC, VS
Children over 12
Wolsey Lodge

Crutchfield Farm makes an ideal place for Britons to spend the night before going on holiday as Gill and Tony offer long-term parking for their guests' cars and give them a ride to Gatwick airport. For visitors to Britain Crutchfield Farm provides an ideal first or last night's stay since it is just ten minutes' drive from the airport, though away from the noise of the flight paths. There has been a farm here since the 1300s, with the present large home evolving since the 15th century—it was once owned by Queen Katherine of Aragon and was presented to her by Henry VIII as a wedding present. Exposed beams throughout reflect the period of the house. Relax in the comfortable sitting room or stroll through the 10 acres of gardens with swimming pool and tennis court overlooking a lake. The largest bedroom, whose tall, exposed-beam ceiling stretches up to the rafters, can accommodate a family of four and has a small shower room tucked into a corner of the room. A delightful double-bedded room has an en suite bathroom while a lovely twin-bedded room has its private bathroom across the hall. Breakfast is the only meal served, and guests often go to the pub just down the road for dinner. Visitors can take the train from Gatwick into London for the day (½ hour) or visit Chartwell, Churchill's home, (½ hour) or Hever Castle (40 minutes). *Directions:* From Gatwick take the A23 towards Redhill to the A217 Reigate road. Pass The Black Horse pub on the right and take the little lane to the left (Crutchfield Lane)—the house is on the left after half a mile.

CRUTCHFIELD FARM
Owners: Gill & Tony Blok
Crutchfield Lane
Hookwood, nr Horley
Surrey RH6 0HT, England
Tel: (01293) 863110, Fax: (01293) 863233
E-mail: tonyblok@compuserve.com
3 rooms, 2 en suite
£37.50 per person
Closed Christmas, Credit cards: none
Children welcome, No-smoking house

The rector of Hopesay was quite the lord of the manor, with most of the buildings in this tiny hamlet falling under his domain: the 12th-century church of St. Mary, the grand, 17th-century rectory, servants' cottages, stables, barns, and a school. Parishioners came from outlying farms and villages. However grand the former rector's lifestyle may have been, the house can never have looked lovelier than it does today. Relax by the log fire in the beautiful drawing room and admire the garden vista of mature copper beeches, Norway maples, azaleas, and rhododendrons. Enjoy a lovely dinner and breakfast round the long refectory table overlooking Hopesay Hill (NT). Equally delightful views are offered from the three very attractively decorated bedrooms. There are excellent country walks from the house and locally to Offa's dyke and the Long Mynd. Historical remains, hill forts, and castles abound (nearby Stokesay and Ludlow are a must). Guests often spend a day visiting the Ironbridge Gorge museums, while antiquers head to Ludlow and Shrewsbury. *Directions:* Leave the A49 at Craven Arms and take the B4368 to Clun. At Aston-on-Clun turn right over a small humpback bridge by the Flag Tree (literally a tree festooned with flags). The Old Rectory is on your left, next to the church, after 1 mile.

THE OLD RECTORY
Owners: Roma & Michael Villar
Hopesay
Craven Arms
Shropshire SY7 8HD, England
Tel: (01588) 660245, Fax: (01588) 660502
3 rooms
£35 per person, dinner £20
Closed Christmas & New Year
Credit cards: none
Children over 12
No-smoking house

Sitting at the heart of the peaceful village of Hornton, the 17th-century Manor House is the exquisite home of Vicki and Malcolm Patrick and their three children. The elegant drawing room is set aside for guests' use and meals are taken in the beautifully appointed beamed dining room. Winter, decked out in soft tones of peach, is a delightful bedroom. Sweet peas decorate the bed linen in the Crow's Nest, an aptly named, snug attic room with exposed stone walls and a huge beam running across its floor. Across the courtyard, part of the stables has been converted into an adorable, two-bedroom, one-bath cottage that can be rented as self catering or on a bed-and-breakfast basis. Vicki is happy to prepare dinner when ordered in advance or directs guests to one of the numerous nearby village pubs that serve excellent food. Guests are welcome to swim in the swimming pool. Nearby Upton House, with its amazing collections of old masters paintings, Brussels tapestries, porcelain figures, and 18th-century furniture, is popular, as is the glorious Elizabethan home, Charlecote, and its surrounding park. *Directions:* From Banbury follow signposts for Stratford until you reach traffic lights where the Stratford road goes left. Carry straight on the B4100 towards Warmington for half a mile then turn left for Horley and Hornton. In Horley turn right towards Hornton and in 2 miles turn left for Hornton. Drive down the hill and the manor house is on the left just past the post box on the verge and opposite the village school.

THE MANOR HOUSE
Owners: Vicki & Malcolm Patrick
The Green, Hornton, Banbury
Oxfordshire OX15 6BZ, England
Tel & fax: (01295) 670386
www.karenbrown.com/england/themanorhouse.html
4 rooms, 2 en suite
£35–£45 per person, dinner £25
Open all year
Credit cards: none
Children welcome

Behind the tile-hung façade of Rixons lies a home that dates back to Tudor times, full of beams and low ceilings, with an inglenook fireplace and a snug, paneled study. Enjoy breakfast round the long refectory table and chat with Geoffrey and Jean about the local pubs that they recommend for dinner. The galleried guestroom is open to the rafters with its bedroom downstairs and a sitting room and the bathroom on the balcony above. Honey-colored beams, country-pine furniture, and sprigged bedcovers make the twin-bedded room, tucked under the eaves, a delight. Horsted Keynes has a lovely old church built as a replica of one in Cahagnes, France by a Norman nobleman after the Battle of Hastings. There are two village pubs serving food a few minutes' walk away. On weekends and in the summer, vintage steam trains run between Horsted Keynes and Sheffield Park, which is especially beautiful in spring. Other lovely gardens include Nymans, Leonardslee, and Wakehurst Place. *Directions:* From the M25 take the M23 south, exiting at junction 10 on the A264 towards East Grinstead. At the second roundabout turn right on the B2028 and go about 6 miles through Ardingly. Take the left turning signposted Horsted Keynes and Danehill. In Horsted Keynes turn right into the Lewes Road—Rixons is the second house on the right.

RIXONS
Owners: Jean & Geoffrey Pink
Lewes Road
Horsted Keynes
West Sussex RH17 7DP, England
Tel: (01825) 790453, Fax: none
www.karenbrown.com/england/rixons.html
2 rooms
£30 per person
Closed Christmas & New Year
Credit cards: none
Children over 12
No-smoking house

Set in a valley carved by a stream rushing down from high, bleak moorlands, Hutton le Hole is a cluster of pale stone houses, a picturesque village in the heart of the spectacular North Yorkshire Moors National Park. The lintel above the Hammer and Hand's doorway declares the date of the house, built as a beer house for the iron workers, as 1784. Now it is home to Ann, a journalist, and John, once a London policeman, and their family, who happily welcome visitors to their guesthouse. Dinner is available Friday to Monday, served in a small paneled dining room. The gentle tick of a huge grandfather clock and the crackle of a blazing log fire welcome you to the sitting room, where a television is available for guests' use. A steep, narrow staircase leads to three snug bedrooms, each prettily decorated. Additional bedrooms are found in the adjacent cottage. Hutton le Hole houses the Ryedale Folk Museum, which is well worth a visit. York is less than an hour's drive away. *Directions:* Take the A170 from Thirsk towards Pickering. The left-hand turn to Hutton le Hole is signposted just after Kirbymoorside. The Hammer and Hand is at the heart of the village.

HAMMER AND HAND GUEST HOUSE
Owners: Ann & John Wilkins
Hutton le Hole
York
North Yorkshire YO62 6UA, England
Tel: (01751) 417300, Fax: (01751) 417711
7 rooms
£25–£27 per person, dinner £15
Open all year
Credit cards: MC, VS
Children welcome
No-smoking house

The highlight of a stay at the Old Windmill is to experience the welcome and gracious hospitality of its resident owners, Sheila and Mike Dale. Set on a tranquil 2-acre parcel, this interesting old building's structure and character have evolved with its various uses. It originated as a mill during the 1840s and the turret-like tower still dominates the structure. In 1906 it was converted to a residence with the dramatic addition of a two-story wing, then later the Dales further extended the house and added many luxurious features. From the entry area you pass through the kitchen to a very modern breakfast room enclosed by glass with views out to the Malvern Hills. From the entry climb the turret stairs to the dining room whose windows are set in the curvature of the turret walls. A few steps up from here is the cozy Worcester Room, whose color scheme in beiges and peach is pretty against the exposed whitewash of the timbered walls. Off the turret stair is the most popular room, the Malvern Room, with a pretty, soft-yellow pattern of fleur-de-lys and a wall of windows looking across to the Malvern Hills. Downstairs is the Stratford Room whose high windows look out to the stone walls of the surrounding quarry—this is not the room to choose if you want a view. Set under dark beams, the deep rose of the spread contrasts with the zebra chairs. *Directions:* Inkberrow is on the A422 between Worcester and Stratford. In the center of town, turn up Stonepit Lane and turn left at the first crossroads. The Old Windmill is the third property on the right.

THE OLD WINDMILL   New
Owners: Sheila & Mike Dale
Withybed Lane, Inkberrow
Worcestershire WR7 4JL, England
Tel & fax: (01386) 792801
E-mail:sheila@theoldwindmill.demon.co.uk
3 rooms
£45 per person, dinner £21
Open all year, Credit cards: VS
Children by arrangement, No-smoking house
Wolsey Lodge

No need to request a room with a view at Nonsuch House, for every room offers a spectacular panorama of the sheltered harbor of Dartmouth with its castle, houses tumbling down the wooded hillside to the river, and yachts tugging at their moorings. The view won the hearts of Patricia, Geoffrey, and Christopher Noble (a parents-and-son trio) who decided to reduce the workload involved in running an upscale country house hotel (Langshott Manor) and concentrate on the aspect of the hospitality business that gives them most satisfaction—looking after their guests. After a day of sightseeing, enjoy a set, three-course dinner in the conservatory and watch the activity in the harbor below. Bedrooms, which come with a choice of queen, king or twin beds, are absolutely delightful and each is accompanied by an immaculate modern bathroom. A fun day trip involves taking a ferry and steam train into Paignton. On Tuesdays in summer you can take the ferry to Totnes and stroll around the market admiring the townsfolk in their colorful Elizabethan costumes. *Directions:* From Totnes take the A385 to Paignton then the A3022 Brixham/A379 Dartmouth road after passing the Ford Garage turn immediately right on the A379. Just after passing the Hillhead garage fork left for Kingswear and on reaching the town enter the one-way system, turning left onto the Higher Contour Road. Go to the top of the hill and on down Ridley Hill. As you round a left-hand bend look for parking—Nonsuch House is below you at the hairpin bend.

NONSUCH HOUSE
Owners: Patricia, Geoffrey, & Christopher Noble
Church Hill
Kingswear, Dartmouth
Devon TQ6 0BX, England
Tel: (01803) 752 829, Fax: (01803) 752 357
5 rooms, 4 en suite
£37.50 per person, dinner £15
Open all year
Credit cards: none
Children over 10

The magnificent scenery of the Lake District, the Yorkshire Dales, and Hadrian's Wall are within easy driving distance of Hipping Hall, so visitors can easily justify a stay of several days in Jocelyn and Ian Bryant's comfortable home. (There are reduced half-board rates for guests staying more than two nights.) Guests enjoy pre-dinner drinks in the conservatory linking the main part of the house to the Great Hall where dinner is served. A soaring, beamed ceiling and a broad-oak-plank floor provide an impressive setting for the excellent five-course meal served around one large table where guests are looked after by Ian while Jocelyn creates in the kitchen. Ian selects wine to complement each course. The bedrooms are named after local hills and dales, and all are comfortably and very tastefully furnished, often with lovely old pieces bought at local auctions. Each has its own sparkling new, well-equipped bathroom. The 3 acres of garden are a delight and feature a large expanse of lawn set up for croquet and a kitchen garden providing many of the vegetables enjoyed at dinner. Two suites, named Emily and Charlotte after the Brontë sisters who attended school in Cowan Bridge, occupy a courtyard cottage. Each has a kitchen and living room downstairs, bedroom and bathroom upstairs. *Directions:* Leave the M6 at junction 36 and follow the A65 through Kirkby Lonsdale towards Skipton. Hipping Hall is on the left, 3 miles after Kirkby Lonsdale.

HIPPING HALL
Owners: Jocelyn & Ian Bryant
Cowan Bridge
Kirkby Lonsdale
Cumbria LA6 2JJ, England
Tel: (015242) 71187, Fax: (015242) 72452
E-mail: hippinghal@aol.com
www.karenbrown.com/england/hippinghall.html
5 rooms & 2 suites
£44–£53 per person, dinner £24
Open Mar to Nov, Credit cards: MC, VS
Children over 12

Lavenham with its lovely timbered buildings, ancient guildhall, and spectacular church is the most attractive village in Suffolk. The Great House on the corner of the market square, a 15th-century building with an imposing 18th-century façade, houses a French restaurant-with-rooms run by Martine and Regis Crepy. Dinner is served in the oak-beamed dining room with candlelight and soft music and is particularly good value for money from Monday to Friday when a fixed-price menu is offered. On Saturday you dine from the à-la-carte menu and on Sunday evenings the restaurant is open only if guests are staying. In summer you can dine al fresco in the flower-filled courtyard. There are four large bedrooms, all with a lounge or a sitting area and bathroom. One has a second bedroom. Architecturally the rooms are divinely old-world, with sloping plank floors, creaking floorboards, little windows, and a plethora of beams. Enjoy the village in the peace and quiet of the evening after the throng of daytime summer visitors has departed. Next door, Little Hall is furnished in turn-of-the-century style and is open as a museum. Farther afield are other historic villages such as Kersey and Long Melford, and Constable's Flatford Mill. *Directions*: Lavenham is on the A1141 between Bury St. Edmunds and Hadleigh.

THE GREAT HOUSE
Owners: Martine & Regis Crepy
Market Place
Lavenham
Suffolk CO10 9QZ, England
Tel: (01787) 247431, Fax: (01787) 248007
E-mail: greathouse@clara.co.uk
www.karenbrown.com/ews/greathouse.html
5 rooms
£41–£51 per person, dinner £18.95–£30
Closed Jan
Credit cards: all major
Children welcome

Buckton is a cluster of cottages and a couple of farms lining a quiet country lane on the outskirts of the pretty village of Leintwardine in the heart of the Marches, once an area of much inter-fiefdom feuding and armed conflict along the Welsh border. A 12th-century motte (mound) from a motte and bailey castle sits at the bottom of Yvonne and Hayden Lloyd's garden as evidence of the area's turbulent history. The substantial, tall Georgian farmhouse, very typical of those in this area, is a working farm with Hayden working with son Richard raising cattle and sheep and growing cereal. Three attractive bedrooms are found up the steep, broad flight of stairs. The double-bedded room has an en-suite shower room while the two twin-bedded rooms have their own private bathrooms across the hall. The Lloyds have an easy, welcoming way with guests that makes visitors feel very much a part of the family. Visiting castles is a popular pastime and they come in all shapes and sizes, from tiny Stokesay to the grandeur of Powys. Yvonne plans a route for guests through the unspoiled black and white timbered villages of neighboring Herefordshire. *Directions:* From Ludlow take the A49 north towards Shrewsbury for 3 miles and turn left on the A4113 towards Knighton. Cross the bridge in Leintwardine and take the first right (still A4113) to Walford (1 mile) where you turn right for Buckton. Follow the narrow lane and Upper Buckton is the second farm on the left.

UPPER BUCKTON
Owners: Yvonne & Hayden Lloyd
Upper Buckton, Leintwardine, nr Craven Arms
Shropshire SY7 0JU, England
Tel: (01547) 540634, Fax: none
3 rooms, 1 en suite
£30–£35 per person, dinner £18
Open all year
Credit cards: none
Children welcome, No-smoking house

Tucked in an unspoilt valley high above the hustle and bustle of the more well-known Lake District tourist routes, this traditional pub lies surrounded by the ruggedly beautiful Lakeland scenery. Built of somber-looking slate in 1872 as a resting place for travelers, the hostelry is still a base for tourists, many of whom come here for the walking. They gather by the bar, the sound of their hiking boots echoing hollowly against the slate floor, poring over maps and discussing the day's activities. By contrast, the carpeted and curtained dining room and lounge with its velour chairs seem very sedate. The Stephenson family pride themselves on the quality of their food and offer a five-course meal in addition to substantial bar meals. Recently refurbished bedrooms maintain the character of a 19th-century inn. For travelers who enjoy prettily decorated, simply furnished, and spotlessly clean rooms with modern bathrooms, the Three Shires fits the bill. Just a few miles away are some of the Lake District's most popular villages: Hawkshead, Ambleside, Coniston, and Grasmere. *Directions:* From Ambleside take the A593, Coniston road, cross Skelwith Bridge, and take the first right, signposted The Langdales and Wrynose Pass. Take the first left to Little Langdale and the Three Shires Inn is on your right.

THREE SHIRES INN
Owners: Stephenson family
Little Langdale
Ambleside
Cumbria LA22 9NZ, England
Tel: (015394) 37215, Fax: (015394) 37127
E-mail: ian@threeshiresinn.com
www.karenbrown.com/england/threeshiresinn.html
10 rooms
£33–£41 per person, dinner £10–£20
Closed Jan
Credit cards: MC, VS
Children welcome

Built in 1673 as a rectory, Landewednack House sits above the 6th-century church and a cluster of cottages that lead down to the rocky inlet of Church Cove at the tip of the Lizard Peninsula, the southernmost spot in England. Restored to a state of luxury unknown to former residents, Landewednack House was purchased by Marion and Peter Stanley who fell in love with the house, its walled garden, and magnificent views. Guests are welcomed with a traditional Cornish tea of scones, clotted cream, and strawberry jam served in the elegant sitting room, secluded garden, or by the sheltered swimming pool. In the evening guests may dine together in the dining room before a log fire in the massive 17th-century fireplace or separately in the beamed morning room. The starched linen coverlets on the polished mahogany half-tester bed in the Yellow Room present a dramatic picture in a room whose floor-to-ceiling bay window frames a lovely view of the garden and the church silhouetted against the sea. Choose the Red Room for its 18th-century four-poster bed or the Chinese Room for its silk-draped king-sized bed that can also be twins. Walk along the clifftops to the adorable village of Cadgwith or visit the many beautiful Cornish gardens. *Directions:* From Helston, take the A3083 to Lizard (do **not** turn right at the first Church Cove sign near Helston). Turn left before entering the village, signposted Church Cove. Take the next left (Church Cove and Lifeboat Station) and Landewednack is on the left.

LANDEWEDNACK HOUSE
Owners: Marion & Peter Stanley
Church Cove, Lizard, Helston
Cornwall TR12 7PQ, England
Tel: (01326) 290909, Fax: (01326) 290192
www.karenbrown.com/england/landewednack.html
3 rooms, 2 en suite
£39–£44 per person, dinner £22.95
Closed Christmas, Credit cards: MC, VS
Children over 16, No-smoking house
Wolsey Lodge

New House Farm sits beside the lane surrounded by green fields beneath rugged Lakeland peaks. Hazel grew up at a hotel and returned here with her young children to provide gracious guest accommodation in this 17th-century farmhouse and transform the barn into a tea room and restaurant. Flagstone floors, beamed ceilings, and old fireplaces are the order of the day in the farmhouse. Hazel prepares a set, five-course dinner, but if you prefer a lighter, less formal meal, walk across to the barn where little tables and chairs are arranged in the old cow stalls, specials are posted on the board, and main courses include quiche, fish, and steak. Upstairs, two of the country-cozy bedrooms offer zip-link beds and en-suite bathrooms while the other two are snug double-bedded rooms with en-suite shower rooms. My favorite room lies a few steps from the house in the former stables—its ground-floor location makes it ideal for those who have difficulty with stairs. New House Farm sits amid the rugged scenery that has made the Lake District such a draw for centuries. Stride up Grasmoor or follow the country lane to Crummock Water and Buttermere from where the road winds and twists over the fells to Rosthwaite, Grange, and Keswick. *Directions:* From exit 40 on the M6 take the A66 past Keswick, and turn left onto the B5292 to Lorton. Follow signs for Buttermere and New House Farm is on your left after half a mile.

NEW HOUSE FARM
Owner: Hazel Hatch
Lorton nr Cockermouth
Cumbria CA13 9UU, England
Tel & fax: (01900) 85404
www.karenbrown.com/england/newhousefarm.html
5 rooms
£38–£48 per person, dinner £22
Open all year
Credit cards: none
Children over 10
No-smoking house

This endearing cottage dates back to the early 14th century when it was home to a yeoman farmer. With its little upstairs windows peeking out from beneath a heavy thatched roof and its timber-framed wall fronted by a flower-filled garden, Loxley Farm presents an idyllic picture. The picture-book ambiance is continued inside where guests breakfast together round a long table in the low-beamed dining room. Accommodation is across the garden in the converted 17th-century thatched, half-timbered cart barn with two modern, functional suites. The Hayloft Suite has vaulted ceilings, bedroom, bathroom, sitting room, and small kitchen, while the more desirable Garden Suite, has bedroom, bathroom, and garden room whose semi-circular glass walls look over the orchard, lawns, and house. Breakfast is the only meal served in the farmhouse dining room and for dinner guests often walk into Loxley or go to The Bell in Alderminster. A quiet back road brings you into the center of Stratford-upon-Avon (4 miles). Here there are historical timbered buildings to investigate, lovely shops, and the Royal Shakespeare Theatre. In nearby Shottery is Anne Hathaway's picture-book cottage. Warwick Castle and Coventry Cathedral are both easily visited from Loxley. *Directions:* Loxley is signposted off the A422 Stratford-upon-Avon to Banbury road about 4 miles from Stratford on the left. Go through the village to the bottom of the hill, turn left (Stratford-upon-Avon), and Loxley Farm is the third house on the right.

LOXLEY FARM
Owners: Anne & Rod Hornton
Loxley
Warwickshire CV35 9JN, England
Tel: (01789) 840265, Fax: (01789) 840645
www.karenbrown.com/england/loxleyfarm.html
2 rooms
£30–£33 per person
Closed Dec
Credit cards: none
Children welcome

Set in a sheltered valley in the center of Exmoor National Park, this farm complex encompasses several 14th-century barns and a 200-year-old farmhouse set round a cobbled courtyard. Hens, guinea fowl, and peacocks complete the idyllic countryside picture. Three very nice bedrooms are found in the sturdy farmhouse: the attractive twin-bedded room is my favorite because of its spaciousness, airy decor, two comfortable armchairs, and lovely countryside views. The same view is shared by the adjacent four-poster room, while a small double-bedded room is found at the back of the house. If you are traveling with younger children, you might want to stay on a bed-and-breakfast basis in one of the self-catering cottages in the ancient barns. Ann provides a set three-course candlelit dinner and guests are welcome to bring their own wine to accompany their meal. Guests can fish in the Durbins' trout lake or go salmon-fishing on the nearby Exe and Barle rivers. Exmoor has delightful little unspoilt villages nestling in wooded valleys, rugged moorlands where sheep and ponies graze, and a coastline with the delightful seaside towns of Lynton and Lynmouth and the quaint little village of Porlock Weir. *Directions:* Exit the M5 at junction 25, take the A358 (Minehead road) for 5 miles, bypassing Bishops Lydeard, and turn left on the B3224 to Wheddon Cross. Go straight across the main street of the village and Cutthorne is on your left after 3 miles.

CUTTHORNE
Owners: Ann & Philip Durbin
Luckwell Bridge, Wheddon Cross
Somerset TA24 7EW, England
Tel & fax: (01643) 831255
www.karenbrown.com/england/cutthorne.html
3 rooms, 2 cottages
£25–£31 per person, dinner £15
Open all year
Credit cards: none
Children over 12 in house, any age in cottages
No-smoking house

The Salweys of Shropshire can trace their lineage hereabouts back to 1216 and The Lodge has been in their family since it was built in the early 1700s, but it is definitely not a formal place. Hermione puts guests at ease, encouraging them to feel as though they are friends of the family, and enjoys pointing out the architectural details of the house and explaining who's who amongst the family portraits. In the evening, guests gather in the morning room and help themselves to drinks from the honesty bar before going into dinner at a spectacular long table made of burled wood, made especially for the house. Up the grand staircase the three large bedrooms are most attractive: Chinese has a suite of furniture painted in an Asian motif, Roses is a large double with an enormous bathroom, and The Yellow Room is a large twin with its bathroom across the hall. The large garden, woodland, and farmland make this an ideal place for walking. The nearest tourist attraction is the medieval town of Ludlow with its old inns, alleyways of antique shops, Norman castle, and riverside walks. *Directions:* Leave Ludlow over Ludford Bridge traveling south. After 1½ miles turn right on the B4361 signposted Richards Castle. After 400 yards turn right through the entrance gates of The Lodge by a curved stone wall, and continue up the long drive to the house.

THE LODGE
Owners: Hermione & Humphrey Salwey
Ludlow
Shropshire SY8 4DU, England
Tel: (01584) 872103, Fax: (01584) 876126
3 rooms, 2 en suite
£40 per person, dinner £20 (wine included)
Open Apr to Oct
Credit cards: none
Children not accepted
No-smoking house
Wolsey Lodge

Ludlow is a charming, compact town of cobbled stone streets rising from the River Teme to its immense Norman Castle, and the most delightful street in town is the splendid upsweep of Lower Broad Street which narrows to the 13th-century Broadgate, the only surviving gatehouse. The architecture of Lower Broad Street runs the gamut from Tudor through Georgian to Victorian and Number Twenty Eight offers you a house of each style, with two en-suite bedrooms in each house. Number Twenty Eight itself is Georgian—you step directly from the street into a cozy parlor with an open fire, book-lined walls, prints, plates, and pictures, and a warm welcome from Patricia and Philip Ross. Guests congregate here for breakfast, which in summer is served on the flower-filled terrace. If you are staying up the road, you have your choice of eating here or preparing yourself a Continental breakfast from your well-stocked refrigerator. Broadgate Mews is two tiny Tudor cottages combined to form a secluded haven, while the delightful Westview is a restored Victorian terrace home offering especially nice bedrooms with brass-and-wrought-iron beds and spacious, very up-to-date bathrooms. Explore the immense Norman castle and wander the lanes with their fine period houses and plethora of book and antique shops. *Directions:* Arriving from the south, fork left off the A49 onto the B4361 signposted Ludlow south and Richards Castle. Cross the river and go straight into Lower Broad Street. There is unrestricted parking on the street.

NUMBER TWENTY EIGHT
Owners Patricia & Philip Ross
Lower Broad Street
Ludlow, Shropshire SY8 1PQ, England
Tel: (01584) 876996, Fax: (01584) 87860
E-mail: ross.no28@btinternet.com
www.karenbrown.com/england/numbertwentyeight.html
6 rooms
£35–£40 per person
Open all year, Credit cards: MC, VS
Children welcome, No-smoking house

Set in the gently rolling countryside of the Yorkshire Wolds between York and the North York Moors National Park, Newstead Grange is ideally located for exploring these popular tourist destinations and the coastal towns of Whitby and Scarborough. Pat and Paul Williams forsook their careers as teachers to purchase a spacious Georgian home and open it as a bed and breakfast. Guests have two comfortable sitting rooms, one resplendent with grand piano in the large bay window overlooking the garden. Pat enjoys cooking and while there are no choices on her daily menu, she tries to avoid foods guests dislike. Many of her vegetables come from the large garden. Upstairs, the bedrooms, all named after former owners, range in size from the spaciousness of Pickering with its half tester bed to two very snug little rooms in a tiny cottage annexed to the house. Castle Howard is just 8 miles away—one look at its immense façade reflecting in a broad lake and you can understand why it took 27 years to build. It isn't really a castle at all but one of England's grandest homes, as impressive inside as out, full of fine furniture and paintings. There is also a wealth of more intimate less imposing homes to visit such as Sledmere House near Malton and Duncombe Park in nearby Helmsley. *Directions:* Follow signs for Beverley (B1248) out of Malton and half a mile beyond the last houses you find Newstead Grange on your left opposite a road sign for Settrington.

NEWSTEAD GRANGE
Owners: Pat & Paul Williams
Beverley Road
Norton on Derwent
Malton
North Yorkshire YO17 9PJ, England
Tel: (01653) 692502, Fax: (01653) 696951
8 rooms
£34.50–£38.50 per person, dinner £18.50
Open mid-Mar to mid-Oct, Credit cards: MC, VS
Children over 10
No-smoking house

Conjecture has it that Thomas Hardy used Old Lamb House (then the Lamb Inn) as Rollivers Tavern in *Tess of the d'Urbervilles*. Jenny and Ben continue the tradition of hospitality by offering accommodation to guests in two large front bedrooms that share a bathroom. Guests use the front door (family members use the kitchen door) and atop the curving staircase there's a sitting area with two armchairs and lots of tourist information. Jenny finds that most guests prefer to relax in their bedrooms, both of which contain comfortable, old-fashioned armchairs. The Pink Room is decked out in soft pinks with matching flowery bed-linen and drapes, while the Gray Room is outfitted in soft blue-grays and offers lovely views of the garden with its stately cedar tree. Guests usually drive the short distance to the White Horse or the Blackmore Vale pubs for dinner. Alternatively, there are several restaurants nearby. Dorset abounds in country lanes that lead to pretty villages such as Milton Abbas and Cerne Abbas with its club-wielding giant carved into the chalk hillside. Shaftesbury has many steep roads running down into Blackmore Vale, the most famous being cobbled Gold Hill. *Directions:* From Shaftesbury take the A30 towards Exeter for 4 miles to East Stour. Turn left on B3092 to Marnhull (3 miles) and go half a mile beyond Marnhull church where you turn right at the triangle of grass with a signpost and into Old Lamb House's driveway.

OLD LAMB HOUSE
Owners: Jenny & Ben Chilcott
Marnhull
Dorset DT10 1QG, England
Tel: (01258) 820491, Fax: (01258) 821464
E-mail: ben@bcaviation.demon.co.uk
www.karenbrown.com/england/oldlambhouse.html
2 rooms, not en suite
£20 per person
Closed Christmas & New Year
Credit cards: none
Children welcome, No-smoking house

Middleham is an attractive town of gray-stone houses sitting beneath the ruins of Middleham Castle. Separated from the cobbled market square by a rose garden, Waterford House is much older than its Victorian exterior suggests. Built as a substantial family home, the house was in recent times divided into two by a husband and wife who wished to live apart but remain in the same village. Now, happily, it is a single house again, the stairways to the bedrooms at either side of the house the only reminders of its days as two homes. These delightful bedrooms, two of which are four-posters, all have an en-suite shower and are furnished, as is the entire house, with lovely old furniture and Everyl and Brian's collections of all things old and interesting. Two double rooms have an extra bed, and families with two children appreciate a further pull-out bed tucked neatly into the corner. An integral part of your stay here is sampling the delicious dinners that Everyl prepares and serves in the antique-packed dining room. The dinner menu changes slightly every night and completely every week and you can dine à la carte or choose an evening-long five-course dinner. Brian is especially proud of his award winning wine list. Waterford House is an ideal central location for exploring the Yorkshire dales. *Directions:* Leave the A1 on the B6267 to Masham and on to Middleham. Waterford House is on your left (on the Leyburn road) just beyond the town's cobbled square.

WATERFORD HOUSE
Owners: Everyl & Brian Madell
19 Kirkgate
Middleham
North Yorkshire DL8 4PG, England
Tel & fax: (01969) 622090 or Fax: (01969) 624020
www.karenbrown.com/england/waterfordhouse.html
5 rooms
£35–£45 per person, dinner £22.50–£29.50
Open all year, Credit cards: MC, VS
Children welcome

"Neighbrook" is a handsome stone manor house in 36 acres of grounds, the elegant country home of the Playfair family who welcome their guests most warmly. Guests enter off the back graveled courtyard through a door distinguished by a brass, mustached sun into a stone-floor entry area. The guest salon is beautiful. A grouping of rose-colored sofas is set around a large open fireplace and large windows look out on two sides to the front lawn and gardens. Guestrooms are found up a back staircase. The front corner room has a double bed and en-suite bathroom with a marvelous old pine tub, soft pink-and-blue floral fabric, and gorgeous views. A cozy single room with washbasin shares a bath at the end of the hall with the Playfair children (when they are in residence—and guests are favored with first use!). Up more stairs you find a handsome double-bedded room with steps up to a spacious sitting room containing two more single beds and a bathroom looking out to the back. Dining with the Playfairs (by arrangement) is a special treat. Their dining room is elegant: one long trestle table runs the length of the room encircled by handsome windows curtained in colors of soft yellow, cream, and green. *Directions:* Travel north from Moreton in Marsh for three miles on the A429 towards Stratford. Turn west on the road signed Aston Magna then right on the road just in front of the village's first building and travel a short distance to the signed entry gates of "Neighbrook."

"NEIGHBROOK"   **New**
Owners: Camilla & John Playfair
Aston Magna
Moreton in Marsh
Gloucestershire GL56 9QP, England
Tel: (01386) 593232, Fax: (01386) 593500
E-mail: johnplayfair@neighbrook.freeserve.co.uk
3 rooms, 2 en suite
£38 per person, dinner £24
Closed Christmas
Credit cards: MC, VS
Children welcome, Wolsey Lodge

Mungrisdale is one of the few unspoilt villages left in the Lake District and is made up of a pub, an old church, and a cluster of houses and farms set at the foot of rugged, gray-blue crags. Do not confuse The Mill with the adjoining pub, The Mill Inn: drive through the car park of the inn to reach private parking for this cozy hotel. Rooms are of cottage proportions: a small lounge with comfy chairs gathered round a blazing log fire, a cozy dining room where each small oak table is set with blue napkins, candles, willow-pattern china, and a tiny flower arrangement, and nine small bedrooms with matching draperies and bedspreads. Most visitors are drawn here for the dinners prepared by Eleanor. Dinner consists of an appetizer followed by a tasty homemade soup served with soda bread (the latter a popular fixture on the menu), a main course (with a vegetarian alternative), dessert, and cheese and biscuits. Bookings only for bed and breakfast are not usually accepted. The Lake District is a beautiful region, popular with walkers and sightseers alike. Some of its premier villages are Coniston, Hawkshead, Sawrey (home of Beatrix Potter), Ambleside, and Grasmere. *Directions:* Leave the M6 at junction 40 and take the A66 towards Keswick for 10 miles. The Mill is 2 miles north of this road and the signpost for Mungrisdale is midway between Penrith and Keswick.

THE MILL HOTEL
Owners: Eleanor & Richard Quinlan
Mungrisdale
Penrith
Cumbria CA11 0XR, England
Tel: (017687) 79659, Fax: (017687) 79155
www.karenbrown.com/england/themillhotel.html
9 rooms, 7 en suite
£55–£72 per person dinner, B & B
Open Mar to Nov
Credit cards: none
Children welcome

In her younger years Beatrix Potter used to visit Ees Wyke House with her family. Now it is a very pleasant hotel run by Mag and John Williams who have painted and decorated the house from top to bottom in a comfortable style. John, a former cookery teacher at a catering college, enjoys cooking and his dinner menu always offers choices of starter, main course, and dessert. Dinner is taken in the large dining room with glorious views across the countryside. The bedrooms have tall windows framing gorgeous countryside views and many overlook nearby Esthwaite Water. Tucked under the eaves, two airy, spacious attic bedrooms have super views: one has a bathroom en suite while the other has a private bath just next door. The other bedrooms also have a mix of en-suite and adjacent bathroom arrangements. The smallest bedroom, on the ground floor, is reserved for visitors who have difficulty with stairs but unfortunately has no view. A short stroll up the village brings you to Hill Top Farm where Beatrix Potter wrote several of her books. Walks abound in the area and the more oft-trod Lakeland routes are easily accessible by taking the nearby ferry across Lake Windermere. *Directions:* From Ambleside take the A593 towards Coniston. After about a mile turn left on the B5286 to Hawkshead. Skirt Hawkshead village and follow signs for the ferry. Ees Wyke House is on the right just before Sawrey.

EES WYKE COUNTRY HOUSE HOTEL
Owners: Mag & John Williams
Near Sawrey
Hawkshead, Ambleside
Cumbria LA22 0JZ, England
Tel & fax: (015394) 36393
www.karenbrown.com/england/eeswykecountryhousehotel.html
8 rooms, 6 en suite
£60 per person dinner bed & breakfast
Open Mar to Dec
Credit cards: AX
Children over 10

The quiet, narrow country lane that runs in front of Fosse Farmhouse is the historical Fosse Way, the road built by the Romans to connect their most important forts from Devon to Lincolnshire. Although the farmhouse's roadside appeal is diminished by worn flags and the yard cluttered with collectibles, inside, Caron Cooper has furnished her rooms with great flair using soft colors and enviable country-French antiques in every room. Charming knickknacks and country china adorn much of the sitting and breakfast rooms and most pieces are for sale. Upstairs, there are three extremely comfortable guest bedrooms. My favorite was the Pine Room with its mellow pine furniture and especially spacious, luxuriously equipped bathroom. Across the courtyard, the ground floor of the stables has been converted to a tea room and restaurant. On the floor above, three cottage-style bedrooms are stylishly decorated in white on white. With advance notice, Caron enjoys preparing an imaginative, three-course dinner, and is happy to cater to vegetarian palates. At Christmas Caron offers a three-day festive holiday. This tranquil countryside setting is within an easy half-hour's drive of Bath, Bristol, Tetbury, and Cirencester, and the picture-perfect village of Castle Combe is also nearby. *Directions:* Exit the M4 at junction 17 towards Chippenham, turn right on the A420 (Bristol road) for 3 miles to the B4039 which you take around Castle Combe to The Gib where you turn left opposite The Salutation Inn. Fosse Farmhouse is on your right after 1 mile.

FOSSE FARMHOUSE
Owner: Caron Cooper
Nettleton Shrub, Nettleton, Chippenham
Wiltshire SN14 7NJ, England
Tel: (01249) 782286, Fax: (01249) 783066
E-mail: caroncooper@compuserve.com
www.karenbrown.com/england/fossefarmhouse.html
6 rooms
£55–£65 per person, dinner £25
Open all year, Credit cards: all major
Children welcome

Sitting at the head of Wensleydale, Newton le Willows is a very quiet village off the beaten track—a cluster of houses, a pub, and The Hall, home to Oriella Featherstone. Oriella is just as flamboyant as her name suggests and her house is decorated like herself, in a graciously extravagant manner. Artfully draped curtains cascading to the floors hang from all the windows and many of the doors. Sofas are piled with plump cushions, plants trail from pots, and grand flower arrangements grace lovely pieces of furniture, while the dining table is set in the evening with silver service enhanced by twinkling candlelight. Relax in the comfortable drawing room or curl up by the fire in the intimate snug. Oriella has five bedrooms though she never takes more than six guests. All are decorated lavishly and vary in size from spacious to grand (the suite that spans the house). Nearby eating places offer food ranging from inexpensive to some of the best you will find in Britain. Within a half hour's drive of this lovely part of Yorkshire are Middleham with its racing stables and ruined castle of Richard II, Bolton Castle where Mary Queen of Scots was held captive, and the ruins of Jervaulx and Fountains abbeys. *Directions:* Leave the A1 at Leeming Bar taking the A684 to Bedale. At the main street turn right and half a mile out of town take the first left, signposted Newton le Willows. Continue to the T-junction and turn right. At the Wheatsheaf Inn turn left and right into The Hall's driveway.

THE HALL
Owner: Oriella Featherstone
Newton le Willows, nr Bedale
Yorkshire DL8 1SW, England
Tel: (01677) 450210, Fax: (01677) 450014
www.karenbrown.com/england/thehall.html
5 rooms
£40–£50 per person, dinner £25
Open all year
Credit cards: none
Children over 13

This 17th-century former woolen mill deep in the heart of the Devon countryside is now the most welcoming of casual country hotels run with great style by Hazel Phillips and Peter Hunt. It's an informal spot where Peter greets you in the flagstoned hallway and shows you up to your room, encouraging you to make yourself thoroughly at home. After a drink in the bar when Peter passes out the menus, with three choices for each of the three courses, you are shown into the little dining room with its pine tables and chairs set before a massive inglenook fireplace (dinner with reservations Tuesday to Sunday). Upstairs all but one of the cozy bedrooms have snug bathrooms or showers en suite. Peter is an avid beekeeper and after sampling his honey for breakfast, guests often purchase a pot to enjoy back home. Peter's other great interest is his flock of Jacob sheep–woolen garments "fresh from the flock" are often for sale. It's a tremendous place to relax and unwind: sit on the lawn and listen to the burble of the River Bovey flowing alongside, or walk along the river and up on the moors. Birdwatching is a great attraction here. Drogo Castle is just up the road and all the varied delights of Dartmoor National Park are on your doorstep. *Directions:* From Exeter take the A38 to the A382, Bovey Tracy, turnoff. Turn left in Moretonhampstead onto the Princetown road, then immediately left (at the newsagents) to North Bovey. Go straight through the village down the hill and take the first right for the ¼-mile drive to Blackaller.

BLACKALLER
Owners: Hazel Phillips & Peter Hunt
North Bovey
Devon TQ13 8QY, England
Tel & fax: (01647) 440322 (phone to arrange to fax)
www.karenbrown.com/england/blackaller.html
5 rooms, 4 en suite
£37–£39 per person, dinner £22
Open Mar to Dec
Credit cards: none
Children over 12

Set in the picturesque moorland village of North Bovey, frequent winner of the best-kept Dartmoor village award, Gate House has a lovely location just behind the tree-lined village green. The location and warm welcome offered by hosts Sheila and John Williams add up to the perfect recipe for a countryside holiday. The sitting room has an ancient bread oven tucked inside a massive granite fireplace beneath a low, beamed ceiling, and the adjacent dining room has a large oak table in front of an atmospheric old stove. A narrow stairway leads up from the dining room to two of the guest bedrooms, each with a neat bathroom tucked under the eaves. The third bedroom is found at the top of another little staircase, this one off the sitting room, and affords views through a huge copper beech to the swimming pool (unheated), which guests are welcome to use, and idyllic green countryside. Sheila prepares a lovely country breakfast and a four-course evening meal (including vegetarian dishes if requested). Apart from walking on the moor and touring the moorland villages, guests enjoy visiting the many nearby National Trust properties. The Devon coastline is easily accessible and many guests take a day trip into Cornwall, often venturing as far afield as Clovelly. *Directions:* From Exeter take the A38 to the A382, Bovey Tracy, turnoff. Turn left in Mortenhampstead onto the Princetown road, then immediately left again to North Bovey. Go down the lane into the village and Gate House is on the left beyond the Ring of Bells.

GATE HOUSE
Owners: Sheila & John Williams
North Bovey
Devon TQ13 8RB, England
Tel & fax: (01647) 440479
www.karenbrown.com/england/gatehouse.html
3 rooms
£27 per person, dinner £16
Open all year
Credit cards: none
Children over 15, No-smoking house

The sparkling condition of this modern suburban home just 2 miles from the historic heart of Oxford won me over completely. It is conveniently located near a bus stop, but you can also walk or bike into town. Alan, the resident manager, offers a warm welcome and is more than happy to supply guests with maps of the city and point them in the right direction for enjoying all the historic sites. Everything about the bedrooms here is of the highest standards: each is equipped with either a double, twin, or a double and twin beds, and shower room, and is kitted out with a small refrigerator, tea and coffee tray, biscuits, chocolates, and wine glasses—everything you need to make you feel at home. I was particularly impressed by the spacious ground-floor double room (room 7) and rooms 5 and 1, which contain both a double and a single bed. Cotswold House is included in an Inspector Morse detective book, *The Way Through the Woods*. A hearty breakfast (traditional English or vegetarian) is the only meal served. For dinner guests are directed to a local pub, The Kings Arms, or several local restaurants. Leave your car in the forecourt and take the bus into town. Jim suggests that your first port of call be the Oxford Tourist Office, which is also the starting point for informative two-hour walking tours. *Directions:* Cotswold House is on the left, on the A4206, Banbury Road, 2 miles from the center of Oxford.

COTSWOLD HOUSE
Manager: Alan Clarke
363 Banbury Road
Oxford OX2 7PL, England
Tel & fax: (01865) 310558
E-mail: d.r.walker@talk21.com
www.karenbrown.com/england/cotswoldhouse.html
7 rooms
£34 per person
Closed Christmas
Credit cards: MC, VS
Children over 5, No-smoking house

Jean and Jack Langton are the most delightful, attentive hosts and Jean is an accomplished cook who always offers her guests a splendid dinner or, if they prefer a less substantial meal, supper. Jean and Jack dine with their guests around the prettily set dining-room table overlooking their large back garden. Set in a charming countryside village, The Old Rectory began life as two tiny cottages, home to the vicar's coachman and the butler. At the turn of the century the cottages were combined and became the vicarage. Parkham's vicars liked to change residences—there are three old rectories in the village. The Langtons' home is decorated in a light, airy way and while it does not abound in antiques, there is a traditional feel to the house. The largest double bedroom overlooks the garden as does a smaller double room which has its private bathroom across the hall. Guests seek out Jean in the kitchen and chat around the Aga planning their sightseeing excursions, which invariably include the Royal Horticultural Society gardens, Rosemoor in Torrington, and Marwood Hill with its national collection of astilbes. Clovelly, the famous, somewhat over-commercialized village, is a great attraction, as is the Dartington glass factory in Torrington. *Directions:* From Bideford take the A39 south to Horns Cross (Coach and Horses inn) and turn left for Parkham. Bear left by the church and left at the second turning on the right. At The Bell pub turn left and The Old Rectory is on your right halfway down the hill in Rectory Lane.

THE OLD RECTORY
Owners: Jean & Jack Langton
Parkham Nr Bideford
Devon EX39 5PL, England
Tel: (01237) 451443, Fax: none
www.karenbrown.com/england/theoldrectoryparkham.html
3 rooms, 2 en suite
£38–£40 per person, dinner £23
Open Mar to Oct
Credit cards: none
Children over 12, No-smoking house

Take a beautifully furnished 400-year-old farmhouse, add a 500-year-old threshing barn, an old cider shed complete with the press and horse-driven equipment, glorious gardens, acres of apple orchards, and caring hosts and you have ample reason to come to Cokesputt House in the rural Devonshire village of Payhembury. Enjoy a welcoming cup of tea in the drawing room or toast your toes in front of a log-burning fire in the comfortable parlor on a chilly evening. Bring your own wine to accompany dinner round the polished dining table beneath an ancient hewn beam that was once the centerpiece of the farmhouse kitchen, or let Caroline and Angus suggest an excellent pub in one of the nearby villages. Bedrooms are very attractive and you can choose from a spacious twin-bedded, double-bedded, or single room, each accompanied by an en-suite bath or shower room. Angus and Caroline are ardent gardeners who love discussing their own garden and directing guests to the vast number of notable gardens that lie within an hour's drive. Apple orchards on the property enable Angus to produce his own cider using the 100-year-old equipment he has restored in his cider shed. *Directions:* From the M5 exit 28 take the A373 towards Honiton and after 6 miles turn right to Payhembury. In the village turn sharp right opposite the Anglo garage, signposted Tale—Cokesputt House is on the right after 300 yards.

COKESPUTT HOUSE
Owners: Caroline & Angus Forbes
Payhembury
Honiton
Devon EX14 0HD, England
Tel: (0140) 4841289, Fax: none
3 rooms
£32.50 per person, dinner £21
Closed Christmas & Jan
Credit cards: all major
Children over 12, No-smoking house
Wolsey Lodge

Hayes Farmhouse is no longer a working farm but the home of Julia and Thierry Sebline and their friendly Golden Retriever, Flora. The house was built in 1490 as a single-story hall house and expanded over the years to the substantial home you see today. Guests eat before the huge inglenook fireplace and relax in the spacious sitting room overlooking the garden. Julia is happy, with advance notice, to provide dinner and guests can bring their own wine to accompany the meal. A spacious double-bedded room has a small en-suite shower/bathroom and views across the valley to idyllic countryside, while the two other twin-bedded rooms have their private bathroom directly next door. Hayes Farmhouse provides a serene contrast to the bustle of nearby Rye. Just beyond Rye lies Winchelsea, one of the earliest examples of town planning, having been rebuilt in 1277 after being devastated by the marauding French. Inland lies Bodiam Castle, a small, picturesque, castle surrounded by a wide moat, built by Richard II to secure the area against the marauding French. Garden lovers head for Great Dixter and Sissinghurst. Farther afield lies Canterbury. *Directions:* From Rye take the B2089 toward Battle for five miles to Udimore where you turn right, signposted Peasmarsh and Beckley. After a mile turn right into Hayes Lane and Hayes Farmhouse is half a mile down Hayes Lane on the left up the driveway behind the Oast House.

HAYES FARMHOUSE
Owners: Julia & Thierry Sebline
Hayes Lane
Peasmarsh, Rye
East Sussex TN31 6XR, England
Tel: (01424) 882345, Fax: (01424) 882876
E-mail: julia.sebline@virgin.net
3 rooms, 1 en suite
£30 per person, dinner £18
Closed Christmas
Credit cards: none
Children over 6

Penryn is a very much a working town whose main thoroughfare, Broad Street, runs up the hill from the fishing quay. Halfway up the hill, fronting directly onto the street, you find Clare House. Built in the 17th century as an impressive gentleman's residence, it was restored several years ago by Jean and Jack Hewitt who ran the town's newsagents for many years. Jean is chatty and friendly and, while guests have their own spacious sitting room, she often whisks them to her side of the house where she and Jack join them for tea and a chat in their sitting room or in the Victorian conservatory with its hundred-year-old grapevine. Jean finds that having bed-and-breakfast guests has expanded her circle of friends from the town to the world. Bedrooms at the front of the house are particularly large: one has its shower cubicle and sink in the room and the loo across the hall while the other has its private bathroom across the hall. The third bedroom is quietly located at the back of the house and has en-suite facilities. A small refreshment room stocked with tea, coffee, soft drinks, and biscuits is located between the bedrooms. Guests often walk to the Waterfront restaurant or drive to the Pandora, an adorable, thatched inn overlooking Restronguet Creek. *Directions:* From Truro, take the A39 toward Falmouth. Follow the second signpost to Penryn and turn right at the traffic lights on the quay into Broad Street—Clare House is on the left.

CLARE HOUSE
Owners: Jean & Jack Hewitt
20 Broad Street
Penryn
Cornwall TR10 8JH, England
Tel: (01326) 373294, Fax: none
www.karenbrown.com/england/clarehouse.html
3 rooms, 1 en suite
£25–£27 per person
Closed Christmas & New Year
Credit cards: none
Children over 12, No-smoking house

No railroad noise for the lord of the manor in this neighborhood—he lobbied for the Petworth train station to be built beyond earshot, almost 2 miles from town. The last train ran in 1966 and the gingerbread-style Victorian station was cleverly converted to a home several years later. The former waiting room is now the most spacious of sitting rooms, with sofas gathered round the fire and an enormous pine table set for breakfast on cool days. Warmer days find guests breakfasting outside on the platform beside the sweep of lawn that was once the train tracks. Two bedrooms occupy one side of the building—downstairs a brass-and-iron queen-sized bed and spacious modern shower room and upstairs an equally romantic room set beneath a soaring beamed ceiling with high skylights instead of windows. A further four are found in two Edwardian Pullman cars (as used on the Orient Express) sitting in the siding. They have been restored to reflect an era of unrestrained luxury. Breakfast is the only meal served so guests often pop next door to The Badger pub for dinner. Petworth is an ideal base for exploring stately homes (Petworth, Goodwood, Uppark), viewing gorgeous gardens (Westdean, Nymans), and visiting the many interesting old homes that have been relocated to the Weald and Downland Museum. *Directions:* From Guildford take the A3, Portsmouth road, to Milford, the A283 to Petworth, and leave Petworth on the A285, Chichester road. After 1½ miles The Badger pub is on your left. Take the slip road in front of the pub—this leads to The Old Railway Station.

THE OLD RAILWAY STATION
Owners: Lou & Mike Rapley
Petworth
West Sussex GU28 0JF, England
Tel & fax: (01798) 342346
E-mail: mir@old-station.co.uk
6 rooms
£30–£36 per person
Open all year, Credit cards: MC, VS
Children over 16, No-smoking House

Lying in the midst of Hardy country, this imposing manor house surrounded by 5 acres of lovely gardens is the welcoming home of Paddy and Barry Paine who decided to put the house to work for them when their family had grown. Guests are encouraged to make themselves at home in the drawing room and take a refreshing swim in the pool after a warm summer day of sightseeing. Breakfast is the only meal served in the pine breakfast room but Paddy is happy to recommend excellent pubs in the Piddle Valley for dinner. A very large double-bedded room has a separate sitting room and spacious bathroom, while the other double-bedded room is small only by comparison and has its private bathroom across the hall. Walking is popular and there is a good network of excellent footpaths. Dorchester, the Casterbridge of Hardy's novels, lies 4 miles distant. Favorite sightseeing includes Hardy's cottage, Maiden Castle, and Corfe Castle. Salisbury and Shaftesbury are within touring distance. Lulworth Cove, Dirdle Door, and Ringstead Bay are lovely spots to visit on the coast. *Directions:* From Dorchester take the A35 (Bournemouth road) for a quarter of a mile and turn left for Piddlehinton on the B3143. After 4 miles, after a sharp left-hand bend, turn left when the small Muston signpost is on the right. The lane leads to the manor.

MUSTON MANOR
Owners: Paddy & Barry Paine
Piddlehinton
Dorchester
Dorset DT2 7SY, England
Tel & fax: (01305) 848242
2 rooms, 1 en suite
£20–£25 per person
Closed Dec
Credit cards: none
Children over 10
No-smoking house

There was a farm on this site recorded in the Domesday Book of 1086, though the present farm and its outbuildings date from the 1500s. Anthony's family have farmed here for generations and, while he concentrates on all things farming, Lynne concentrates on the upscale bed and breakfast that she runs in a wing of the farmhouse and the converted barns. Her accommodation is not your typical farmhouse style: the rooms I saw were furnished with pastel-painted furniture coordinating with the draperies and bedspreads, giving a light, airy feel. Bathrooms and shower rooms are sparklingly modern and one sports a claw-foot tub and separate shower. Lynne loves to eat out and enjoys discussing dining plans with guests. She also has a folder on restaurants and traditional pubs in the area. Lynne directed us to Tencreek Farm for a scrumptious Cornish cream tea in the prettiest of gardens. If you are planning on staying for a week, consider renting the adorable little cottage for two overlooking the cow pasture. Decorated in vibrant Mediterranean colors, the cottage is excellently equipped for a romantic getaway. The idyllically pretty seaside villages of Fowey, Looe, and Polperro are great attractions as are the National Trust houses of Cotehele and Lanhydrock. *Directions:* From Looe take the A387 signposted Polperro. Before you reach Polperro, Trenderway Farm is signposted to your right.

TRENDERWAY FARM
Owners: Lynne & Anthony Tuckett
Pelynt
Polperro
Cornwall PL13 2LY, England
Tel: (01503) 272214, Fax: (01503) 272991
E-mail: trenderwayfarm@hotmail.com
www.karenbrown.com/england/trenderwayfarm.html
4 rooms
£30–£35 per person
Closed Christmas, Credit cards: MC, VS
Children over 16, No-smoking house

A humorous, tongue-in-cheek "rule" book is found in every bedroom at Bales Mead and woe betide you if you do not comply! The illustrations are drawn by Peter Clover who, with his partner Stephen Blue, runs a very tight ship in their exceptionally attractive home. Guests enjoy a sophisticated sitting room complete with log-burning fireplace and baby grand piano. Upstairs, the bedrooms are named after villages in the Porlock Vale. Selworthy is cool in lemon and blue with outstanding ocean views. Bossington is all in pink, white, and mulberry with a view of the shingle beach and distant headland. Both Selworthy and Bossington have their own private bathrooms. Allerford (a smaller room overlooking the garden and woodlands) is used in conjunction with one of the other rooms by larger parties who do not mind sharing a bathroom. Breakfast is the only meal served (promptly at 9 am)—Stephen and Peter recommend excellent local pubs and restaurants for dinner. In the '50s the house was owned by a well-known horticulturist who filled the garden with specimen plants from all over the world. Just across the lane are vast stretches of shingle beach. Bales Mead is in the hamlet of West Porlock between the pretty village of Porlock and the picturesque harbor of Porlock Weir. Rising behind the house are the vast expanses of Exmoor. *Directions:* From Minehead take the A39 to Porlock, then a right turn to Porlock Weir takes you a short distance to West Porlock, where you find Bales Mead on the left.

BALES MEAD
Owners: Stephen Blue & Peter Clover
West Porlock
Somerset TA24 8NX, England
Tel: (01643) 862565, Fax: (01643) 862544
3 rooms, 2 with private bathrooms
£32 per person
Closed Christmas & New Year
Credit cards: none
Children over 14
No-smoking house

The lifeboatman has been known to deliver guests to Fortitude Cottage when there's an especially high tide. While this is an adventure for visitors, Maggie and Mike take the sea coming up the road as a natural part of living beside the harbor in Old Portsmouth. When she suspects the sea may be paying a visit, Maggie simply removes the rugs from the tile floor in the little downstairs bedroom and mops the floor when the tide ebbs. This attractive room is decorated in pink candy stripes and has a small en-suite shower room. Curl up on the window seat in the airy upstairs sitting room and watch the Isle of Wight ferries and the fishing boats come and go. On the top floor two small pretty bedrooms have tiny en-suite shower rooms (the front room has a harbor view). For dinner, Carol makes suggestions on the pubs and restaurants within walking distance. Take the waterbus (Easter to November) across the harbor to tour Nelson's flagship, *HMS Victory*, Henry VIII's ship, *Mary Rose*, and *HMS Warrior,* an 1861 iron-clad battleship, then go on to the submarine museum. *Directions:* Exit the M27 at junction 12, signposted Portsmouth and ferries. Follow signs for the Isle of Wight car ferry through the center of the town, then look for a brown signpost (at a roundabout) to the cathedral and Old Portsmouth. Pass the cathedral and at the end of the road turn right. Fortitude Cottage is on your left.

FORTITUDE COTTAGE
Owners: Maggie & Mike Hall
51 Broad Street
Old Portsmouth
Hampshire PO1 2JD, England
Tel & fax: (01705) 823748
E-mail: fortcott@aol.com
www.karenbrown.com/england/fortitudecottage.html
3 rooms
£23 per person
Closed Christmas, Credit cards: MC, VS
Children over 12, No-smoking house

The Burgoyne family were people of substance hereabouts for they secured the premier building site in this picturesque Swaledale village and built an impressive home that dwarfs the surrounding buildings. Gone are the days when one family could justify such a large home and now it's a welcoming hotel run by Derek Hickson and Peter Carwardine. Derek makes guests feel thoroughly at home while Peter makes certain that they live up to their motto, "Tis substantial happiness to eat." Peter prepares a fixed-price, four-course meal every evening with plenty of choices for each course. The handsome lounge is warmed by a log fire in winter and full of inviting books on the area. Redmire, being more spacious, is the premier guestroom, while Marrick is a most luxurious four-poster suite. Robes and slippers are provided for the occupants of Keld, Grinton, and Thwaite who have to slip across the hall to their bathrooms. There's abundant scope for walking and driving in this rugged area using Reeth as your base, though you'll be hard pressed to find a lovelier dales view than the one from your bedroom window of stone-walled fields rising to vast moorlands (one bedroom faces the back of the house). Richmond with its medieval castle and the Bowes Museum, near Barnard Castle, with its fine collection of French furniture and porcelain, are added attractions. *Directions:* From Richmond take the A6108 towards Leyburn for 5 miles to the B6270 for the 5-mile drive to Reeth. The Burgoyne Hotel is on the village green.

THE BURGOYNE HOTEL
Owners: Derek Hickson & Peter Carwardine
Reeth
North Yorkshire DL11 6SN, England
Tel & fax: (01748) 884292
www.karenbrown.com/england/burgoyne.html
8 rooms, 5 en suite
£37.50–£70 per person, dinner £23.50
Open Feb 14 to Jan 2
Credit cards: VS
Children welcome

Whashton Springs Farm is a perfect base for exploring the Yorkshire Dales. A five-minute drive finds you at the foot of Swaledale in Richmond, with its cobbled market square and Norman castle perched high above the river. The farm is run by Gordon Turnbull and his two sons who grow corn and potatoes and run a herd of hill cows and sheep. Spring is an especially good time to visit, for the little lambs are kept close to the farm. Fairlie welcomes guests to the farmhouse and offers accommodation within the large sturdy house or in one of the delightfully private bedrooms that open directly onto the courtyard. A wing of the barn has been converted into a most attractive self-catering cottage for families who want to stay for a week. Gordon serves a Yorkshire farmhouse breakfast, giving you an opportunity to ask questions about the farm, and directs guests to local pubs and restaurants in Richmond for dinner. Within an hour you can be in Durham, York, or the Lake District. The Yorkshire Dales are on your doorstep and the North Yorkshire Moors just half an hour distant. *Directions:* From the A1, take the A6136 to Richmond. Turn right at the traffic lights signposted for Ravensworth and follow this road for 3 miles to the farm which is on your left at the bottom of a steep hill.

WHASHTON SPRINGS FARM
Owners: Fairlie & Gordon Turnbull
Richmond
North Yorkshire DL11 7JS
England
Tel: (01748) 822884, Fax: (01748) 826285
www.karenbrown.com/england/whashtonspringsfarm.html
8 rooms
£23–£24 per person
Open Feb to mid-Dec
Credit cards: none
Children over 5

Few English guesthouses offer the ambiance, warmth, and welcome of Mizzards Farm, a lovely 16th-century farmhouse built of stone and brick. The setting is peaceful: the River Rother flows through the 13 acres of gardens and fields and the driveway winds through the large meadowlike front lawn past a small lake. The heart of the house, where breakfast is served, is especially inviting, with one wall filled by a massive inglenook fireplace and a staircase leading up to an open minstrels' gallery. In a newer wing, a sophisticated lounge is nicely furnished with antiques and highlighted by a grand piano. Concerts are held here twice a year. The home was previously owned by an English rock star who converted the largest bedroom into a glitzy, but fun, theatrical showplace with electric curtains operated from the bed on a grand dais and a marble bathroom featuring a double bathtub. The other two guestrooms are smaller and are pleasantly decorated in more traditional decor. Dinner is not served but there are many excellent choices of places to eat nearby. For the athletically minded, Mizzards also has a covered swimming pool for guests' use. *Directions:* From Petersfield take the A272 towards Midhurst. Turn right at the crossroads in Rogate, follow the road for half a mile, cross the narrow bridge over the river, and take the first right on the small lane up to Mizzards Farm.

MIZZARDS FARM
Owners: Harriet & Julian Francis
Rogate
Petersfield
Hampshire GU31 5HS, England
Tel: (01730) 821656, Fax: (01730) 821655
www.karenbrown.com/england/mizzardsfarm.html
3 rooms
£28–£32 per person
Closed Christmas
Credit cards: none
Children over 8
No-smoking house

Rosedale Abbey nestles in a sheltered green valley below the gently rolling moorland. High above the village lies Thorgill, a few houses strung out along a narrow road just beneath the moor. Here you find Sevenford House, a sturdy home built at the turn of the century for the vicar of the village church, and now a private home. Linda found it the perfect place to raise her three elder sons and when they were grown, decided with her partner Ian to open their home to guests. The three large bedrooms are delightfully furnished and each has a snug en-suite shower room. Enjoy a welcoming cup of tea and a chat in the lovely drawing room and browse through the books that highlight the many things to do in this lovely part of Yorkshire. Ride a steam train on the North Yorkshire Moors Railway, visit the vast array of stately homes, explore the lovely villages nestled beneath the moor, and visit the coastside towns of Whitby, Runswick Bay, and Robin Hood's Bay. It's walking country and just above the house you can follow the path of an old railway line that takes you on a spectacular four-hour walk along the moor with views of Rosedale valley. *Directions:* From Pickering take the A170 towards Helmsley for 3 miles, then turn right for the 7-mile drive to Rosedale. Just as you enter the village, turn sharp left and go up the hill to the White Horse Hotel where you turn right (signposted Thorgill). Sevenford House is the first house on your right.

SEVENFORD HOUSE
Owners: Linda Sugars & Ian Thompson
Thorgill, Rosedale Abbey, nr Pickering
North Yorkshire YO18 8SE, England
Tel: (01751) 417283, Fax: (01751) 417505
www.karenbrown.com/england/sevenford.html
3 rooms
£22.50 per person
Closed Christmas
Credit cards: none
Children welcome
No-smoking house

The Roseland Peninsula is one of Cornwall's loveliest areas, a maze of meandering narrow lanes, quaint villages, and exquisite coastal scenery. Set almost in the center of the peninsula you find one of Cornwall's loveliest homes, Crugsillick, a Queen Anne manor house extended in 1710 from an Elizabethan farmhouse, the beautiful home of Rosemary and Oliver Barstow. Guests help themselves to very reasonably priced drinks in the gracious drawing room whose lovely plasterwork ceiling was created by captive French prisoners of the Napoleonic wars. The Barstows often join their guests for dinner. The blue bedroom is very spacious and its king-sized bed can be made into twins. The pink room has a queen-sized bed and its bathroom across the hall, while the yellow room has twin beds and a small shower room. Guests often walk to the beach via a narrow smugglers' lane and enjoy walks along the coast. Gardens abound, the most popular being The Lost Gardens of Heligan, a recently restored garden that had been abandoned for many years. *Directions:* From St. Austell take the B3287 signposted St. Mawes to Tregony where you turn left on the B3275 through Ruan High Lanes. After ¼ mile turn left for Veryan and enter Crugsillick through the third white gate on your right over a cattle grid.

CRUGSILLICK MANOR
Owners: Rosemary & Oliver Barstow
Ruan High Lanes
Cornwall TR2 5LJ, England
Tel: (01872) 501214, Fax: (01872) 501228
E-mail: barstow@adtel.co.uk
www.karenbrown.com/england/crugsillickmanor.html
3 rooms, 2 en suite, 3 cottages
£40–£48 per person, dinner £25
Closed Christmas & New Year
Credit cards: MC, VS
Children over 12
Wolsey Lodge

Rye, a busy port in medieval times, has become marooned 2 miles inland since the sea receded. Once the haunt of smugglers who climbed the narrow cobbled streets laden with booty from France, Rye is now a picturesque town that invites tourists to walk its cobbled lanes. On Rye's most historic street, Jeake's House dates back to 1690 when it was built by Samuel Jeake as a wool storehouse (wool was smuggled to France while brandy, lace, and salt were brought into England). From the street you enter a small reception area which leads to a Victorian parlor and bar which opens up to a large galleried hall, now the dining room, where a roaring log fire blazes in winter. At some point in its history the house was owned by the Baptist Church who built this room as a chapel. From the spacious attic bedroom to the romantic four-poster room and the snug single, no two rooms are alike. All are most attractively decorated and furnished with antiques in keeping with the historical mood of the house. All offer modern amenities such as tea-making trays, television, and telephone and all but two have en-suite bathrooms. Within easy driving distance are Winchelsea, Battle Abbey (built on the site of the Battle of Hastings in 1066), Bodiam Castle, and Sissinghurst Gardens. *Directions:* Rye is between Folkestone and Hastings on the A259. Mermaid Street is the town's main street—park in front to unload and you will be directed to nearby private parking.

JEAKE'S HOUSE
Owner: Jenny Hadfield
Mermaid Street, Rye
East Sussex TN31 7ET, England
Tel: (01797) 222828, Fax: (01797) 222623
E-mail: jeakeshouse@btinternet.com
www.karenbrown.com/england/jeakeshouse.html
12 rooms, 10 en suite
£26.50–£45.50 per person
Open all year
Credit cards: MC, VS
Children over 12

Rye is one of England's most enchanting towns and Little Orchard House is one of Rye's most engaging small bed and breakfasts. The location is ideal, right in the heart of town on a small lane leading off Mermaid Street. Don't miss the inn's discreet sign. An archway frames a most inviting little courtyard faced by a pretty cottage with a red-colored door. Inside there is no formal reception area: registration takes place in the cozy, country-style kitchen, which opens onto a very large old-fashioned walled garden. In one corner rises a red-brick tower, once used by smugglers to signal if the coast was clear. Bedrooms are attractive: Lloyd George is masculine and gracious, the four-poster Garden Room romantic, and the Hayloft cottagey with pine and wicker. The very friendly owners, Sara and Robert, are very involved in the management of their bed and breakfast and personally see that each guest is made welcome and pampered. To learn more about Rye's fascinating history, attend the sound and light show at the Rye Town Model, then set out to explore with a walking tour of the town. *Directions:* Follow signs to the town center and enter via the old Landgate Arch. West Street is the third street on the left off the High Street (ignore the "Authorized traffic only" signs). Park in front to unload and you will be directed to nearby private parking.

LITTLE ORCHARD HOUSE
Owners: Sara Brinkhurst & Robert Bird
West Street
Rye
East Sussex TN31 7ES, England
Tel & fax: (01797) 223831
www.karenbrown.com/england/littleorchardhouse.html
3 rooms
£32–£42 per person
Open all year
Credit cards: MC, VS
Children over 12

Atop the quaint cobbled streets of Rye is the ancient church and churchyard of St. Mary's, surrounded by a square of delightful old houses. Fortunately for visitors to this picturesque town, one of these, The Old Vicarage (a dusty-pink Georgian house with white trim and twin chimneys), is run as a guesthouse by a delightful young couple, Julia and Paul Masters. You can be certain of a proper cuppa here as Julia is a tea-blender and has devised a special blend of tea for her guests. Since Julia and Paul bought The Old Vicarage, they have been constantly upgrading and refurbishing the rooms. All of the guestrooms are decorated with Laura Ashley fabrics: two have contemporary four-poster beds and one has a coronet-style draped headboard. There are also some small rooms tucked under the eaves on the top floor. The garden suite, a large family room with a sitting area, is below stairs. Each of the rooms has color television, hairdryer, and hospitality tray that includes homemade fudge and biscuits—not good for the figure but much appreciated with a cup of tea after sightseeing. The ambiance throughout this bed and breakfast is one of homey comfort. Overnight parking is available in a small private car park nearby. If you write ahead, the Masters will send you a brochure with a map on just how to find them amongst the maze of Rye's streets. Rye deserves a visit of several days to explore its narrow, cobbled streets, shops, and old fortifications. *Directions:* Rye is on the A259 between Folkestone and Hastings.

THE OLD VICARAGE GUEST HOUSE
Owners: Julia & Paul Masters
66 Church Square, Rye
East Sussex TN31 7HF, England
Tel: (01797) 222119, Fax: (01797) 227466
www.karenbrown.com/england/theoldvicarageguesthouse.html
5 rooms
£24–£34 per person
Closed Christmas
Credit cards: none
Children over 8

This lovely Georgian home set in 5 acres of grounds in peaceful countryside offers outstanding accommodations. Rashleigh is an enormous room, its double bed having an artfully draped bedhead matching the curtains and bedspread; Treffry has a 6-foot bed that can be two single beds; and Prideaux has a dainty white four-poster. Each bedroom has an elegant en-suite bathroom with spa bath, tea- and coffee-makings, television, telephone, and a huge umbrella for guests to use during their stay. Guests have their own entrance into a lofty hallway where double doors open up to a vast sitting room all decked out in warm shades of pale green. Beyond lies a sunny conservatory with wicker chairs and little tables set for breakfast, the only meal served. Candid reviews of local restaurants enable guests to decide where they would like to eat, with choices ranging from formal restaurants to a pub on the beach in a smugglers' cove. Outside are vast lawns, a swimming pool, a hot tub, and a paved terrace with spectacular views across rolling countryside. Local attractions include the picturesque town of Fowey, the fishing village of Mevagissey, and National Trust properties such as Lanhydrock. *Directions:* Pass over the Tamar Bridge into Cornwall and follow signs to Liskeard. Take the A390 (St. Austell turnoff), following it through Lostwithiel and into St. Blazey. Cross the railway lines and opposite the Jet garage turn right into Prideaux Road, following it up the hill to Nanscawen on your right.

NANSCAWEN HOUSE
Owners: Fiona & Keith Martin
Prideaux Road, St. Blazey, Par
Cornwall PL24 2SR, England
Tel & fax: (01726) 814488
E-mail: keithmartin@compuserve.com
www.karenbrown.com/england/nanscawenhouse.html
3 rooms
£37–£39 per person
Closed Christmas
Credit cards: MC, VS
Children over 12, No-smoking house

Breathtaking, panoramic views of the Wye Valley open up from Cinderhill House, a pink-washed cottage whose core dates back to the 14th century with additions over the years. Gillie is a warm and friendly hostess who enjoys welcoming guests to her home. Bedrooms in the main house are very prettily decorated and all have tea and coffee trays. An additional attic room with twin beds and a crib is reserved for children so that parents can put their children to bed and go downstairs for dinner. Three self-catering cottages are grouped in the outbuildings—Big Barn has been cleverly oriented so that its four-poster bedroom can be rented either on a B&B basis or as part of a two bedroom cottage. Breakfast is a treat: fruit compotes and cold cereals are followed by hot dishes such as fresh salmon fishcakes and herb omelets, yet Gillie considers dinner her forte! On chilly evenings a crackling log fire invites guests into the large sitting room to enjoy a drink before dinner. Apart from enjoying the peace and quiet of the Wye Valley and the Forest of Dean, guests venture farther afield to Bristol, Cardiff, Gloucester, Cheltenham, Bath, and Hereford. *Directions:* Take the M4 from Bristol towards Chepstow over the old Severn Bridge using the M48 and take exit 22 for Monmouth. Take the A466 for 10 miles, then turn right over the Bigsweir Bridge for St. Briavels. Follow the road up and the house is on the left just before the castle.

CINDERHILL HOUSE
Owner: Gillie Peacock
St. Briavels
Gloucestershire GL15 6RH, England
Tel: (01594) 530393, Fax: (01594) 530098
E-mail: cinderhill.house@virgin.net
www.karenbrown.com/england/cinderhill.html
4 rooms, 3 cottages
£30–£38 per person, dinner £15–£22
Closed Christmas
Credit cards: none
Children welcome

Tim knows how to look after guests: for many years he was the manager (and one of the owners) of Number Sixteen, one of London's splendid little townhouse hotels. After selling his share of the hotel, he came back to his native Devon to run Parford Well. Set within a walled garden, the comfortable house is totally dedicated to guest accommodation while Tim lives in the tiny adjoining cottage. Sink into the oh-so-comfortable sofa in the sitting room and toast your toes before the fire. The decor is of such a high standard that, apart from the smaller proportions of the house, you would think you are in a grand country house hotel. Breakfast is the only meal served round the farmhouse table in the dining room. If you want complete seclusion, ask to eat in the tiny private dining room with grand draperies that once belonged to the Queen Mother and just enough room for a table for two. Upstairs are three delightful small bedrooms, two en suite and one with its private bathroom across the hall. Tim is an expert on where to walk, what to see, and which tea shops and restaurants to frequent. He can suggest enough activities to keep you busy for a fortnight. *Directions:* From Moretonhampstead take the A382 towards Okehampton for 3 miles. Turn right at the Sandy Park crossroads towards Castle Drogo and Parford Well is 100 yards on your left.

PARFORD WELL
Owner: Tim Daniel
Sandy Park
Chagford
Devon TQ13 8JW, England
Tel: (01647) 433353, Fax: none
www.karenbrown.com/england/parfordwell.html
3 rooms, 2 en suite
£23–£28 per person
Open March to Dec 23
Credit cards: none
Children over 8
No-smoking house

A cozy hilltop refuge from winter storms, an outstanding spring, summer, or autumn base for exploring Derbyshire by car or on foot, Dannah Farm is a delightful place for all seasons. The solid Georgian farmhouse is turned over entirely to guests, with two cozy sitting rooms furnished tastefully and delightful cottagey bedrooms. I particularly liked the three suites, two of which have their private entries from the old stableyard. One has a snug sitting room with an open-tread spiral staircase leading to the low-beamed bedroom while the other is a lofty raftered room with a four-poster bed. Another part of the old stables is a convivial bar and country-style restaurant where guests enjoy breakfast and dinner and outside guests are welcomed on Saturday evenings. Adults and children love the animals—the squeaking baby pot-bellied pigs are a great attraction. The Peak District National Park is on your doorstep full of walks, bike trails, and appealing little villages. The stately homes of Haddon Hall and Chatsworth House are well worth a visit. *Directions:* From Belper take the A517 (Ashbourne road) for 2 miles and after the Hanging Gate Inn take the next right (at the top of the hill) to Shottle (1½ miles). Go straight at the crossroads and after 200 yards turn right into Dannah Farm.

DANNAH FARM
Owners: Joan & Martin Slack
Bowmans Lane
Shottle
Belper
Derbyshire DE56 2DR, England
Tel: (01773) 550273, Fax: (01773) 550590
E-mail: reservations@dannah.demon.co.uk
www.karenbrown.com/england/dannahfarm.html
9 rooms, 8 en suite
£35–£55 per person, dinner £17.95
Closed Christmas
Credit cards: MC, VS
Children welcome

Standing apart from the lovely village of Sinnington just beyond its ancient church, Hunters Hill, with its magnificent countryside views, was until recent times the home of the estate manager for the adjacent Sinnington Hall. Jane and John enjoy sharing their home with guests and offer two of their three bedrooms to visitors. A large twin-bedded room has a spacious bathroom separated from the bedroom by a curtained archway. Overlooking the garden and enjoying valley views, the other bedroom has its bathroom across the hall. A snug attic room is available for children. Lovely flower arrangements add to the beautiful dining, sitting, and morning room where guests enjoy breakfast and the magnificent views across the valley to the distant Howard Hills and York. Sinnington lies on the edge of the North Yorkshire Moors National Park with its vast open spaces and little villages in sheltered valleys. The area is rich in historical sites—the ruined abbey of Rievaulx, the castle at Helmsley, and the stately homes of Castle Howard and Duncombe Park. The medieval city of York is half-an-hour's drive away. *Directions:* From Pickering take the A170 (signposted Helmsley) for 4 miles to Sinnington. Turn into the village, cross the green, keeping the village hall (which stands on the green) to your right, turn first right and follow the lane up the hill, bearing right by the church along a farm track which dead-ends at Hunters Hill.

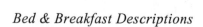

HUNTERS HILL
Owners: Jane & John Orr
Sinnington
York Y06 6SF, England
Tel: (01751) 431196, Fax: (01751) 432976
3 rooms, 1 en suite
£23–£26.50 per person, dinner £23.50
Open all year
Credit cards: none
Children over 12

Gardening is Jane Baldwin's passion—not only does she tend her own 2 acres of exquisite gardens, but she also organizes the National Gardens Scheme in North Yorkshire and can recommend and arrange for you to visit other lovely gardens in the area. Her late-18th-century home is large enough to provide privacy for visitors and family. Guests have their own wing with a dining room (breakfast is the only meal served) and a low-ceilinged, very comfortable sitting room. A double-bedded room has a small en-suite shower room while a more spacious twin-bedded room shares a bathroom with another small single bedroom. Jane always ensures that the bathroom is never shared by guests who are not traveling together. For dinner, guests often wander by the river and across the green to the village pub—if you want to go farther afield, Jane is happy to make recommendations. Sinnington is a lovely, very quiet village just off the main Pickering to Helmsley road, an ideal base for exploring the lovely scenery and villages of the North Yorkshire Moors and making a day trip to the coast to Staithes, Robin Hood's Bay, and Whitby with its impressive abbey ruins. If you're a stately homes person, be sure to visit nearby Castle Howard and Nunnington Hall. *Directions:* From Pickering take the A170 (signposted Helmsley) for 4 miles to Sinnington. Turn into the village, cross the river, and turn right into the lane that leads to Riverside Farm.

RIVERSIDE FARM
Owners: Jane & Bill Baldwin
Sinnington
York YO62 6RY, England
Tel & fax: (01751) 431764
3 rooms, 1 en suite
£22.50–£27.50 per person
Open Apr to Oct
Credit cards: none
Children over 8
No-smoking house

A maze of narrow country roads connects the tiny little villages that dot the rolling countryside just to the south of Shrewsbury. Here you find Lawley House among the cluster of homes that makes up the hamlet of Smethcott. Set atop a hill, this spacious Victorian home faces glorious countryside across a lovely garden full of old-fashioned scented roses. Jackie loves welcoming guests to her home and makes sure that they are well taken care of. Relax in the spacious sitting room and adjacent conservatory that overlooks the garden and the distant Stretton hills. The bedrooms enjoy the same lovely view. One has its bathroom en suite while the other has its spacious bathroom just across the hall. Breakfast is the only meal served round the dining-room table and for dinner guests often go to The Bottle and Glass, just down the lane in Picklescott, or to The Pound, a thatched pub in nearby Leebotwood. Walkers head for the Long Mynd and often take Jackie's one-hour walk that she has outlined from the house. Shrewsbury— with its winding lanes, the castle, its many museums, the market square, and its decorative black-and-white houses—is a "must visit." Farther afield lie Powys Castle and the industrial heritage museums of Ironbridge Gorge. *Directions:* From Shrewsbury take the A49 (towards Leominster) to Dorrington where you turn right for Picklescott. After 3 miles turn left at the crossroads for Smethcott, and ½ mile on is Lawley House, a large cream house straight ahead of you in the fork of two lanes. Smethcott appears on only the most detailed of maps.

LAWLEY HOUSE
Owners: Jackie & Jim Scarratt
Smethcott, nr Church Stretton
Shropshire SY6 6NX, England
Tel: (01694) 751236, Fax: (01694) 751396
www.karenbrown.com/england/lawley.html
2 rooms, 1 en suite
£25–£28 per person
Open all year, Credit cards: none
Children over 12, No-smoking house

The Lynch Country House was built for an attorney and his bride in 1812 and was owned by their family for over a hundred years. Roy Copeland purchased the house with the intention of running a country house hotel: however, when the renovations were complete he decided that a bed and breakfast was more his cup of tea. Consequently guests get country-house-style accommodation at bed-and-breakfast prices and Roy gets time to practice his saxophone and clarinet. Roy encourages guests to enjoy the lovely gardens with their topiary hedges and lake with its resident family of black swans. Bedrooms vary in size from snug rooms under the eaves (Alderley is an especially attractive attic room) to Goldington, a large high-ceilinged room with a grand Georgian four-poster bed. Roy supplies a list of restaurants and pubs in each room along with sample menus but finds that guests usually stroll into the village to The Globe pub. Somerton, long ago the capital of Wessex, is now a substantial village with some interesting shops and pretty streets lined with old stone houses. Glastonbury, the cradle of English Christianity, and Wells with its magnificent cathedral are nearby. Bath is just under an hour away. *Directions:* From the Podimore roundabout on the A303 follow signposts for Langport and Somerton. Join the A372 and turn right after a mile signposted Somerton. Ignore the next two Somerton signs and take the third left by the dairy. Lynch Country House is at the top of the hill by the mini roundabout.

THE LYNCH COUNTRY HOUSE
Owner: Roy Copeland
4 Behind Berry, Somerton
Somerset TA11 7PD, England
Tel: (01458) 272316, Fax: (01458) 272590
www.karenbrown.com/england/thelynchcountryhouse.html
5 rooms, 4 en suite
£24.50–£37.50 per person
Closed Christmas & New Year
Credit cards: all major
Children welcome

Only the most detailed maps pinpoint Curdon Mill in the hamlet of Vellow, but your endeavors to find this lovely valley close to the sea and near the beautiful Quantock hills are rewarded. The approach to the mill skirts Daphne and Richard Criddle's farm. A few years ago they decided to renovate the old water mill on their property, adding a lounge where guests can relax and browse through books describing sights in the area. The mill shaft hangs across the ceiling in the Millers Restaurant, which serves lunch (not Saturday and Monday) and dinner (not Sunday). Of the six bedrooms my favorites are the Stag Room, which was named because deer can sometimes be seen in the fields below the window, and the Walnut Room, named for the walnut bedheads. A small swimming pool is secluded on a terrace beside the mill. Another interesting feature is that the mill is now licensed for civil marriages. This is a rural spot where you can enjoy watching the farm animals, taking walks, trout fishing, or touring nearby gardens. Exmoor National Park is close at hand and Stogumber is a good point from which to visit Bath, Wells, and Glastonbury. *Directions:* Leave the M25 at Taunton, junction 25, and take the A358 towards Williton. Do not turn left until you see Stogumber and Vellow signposted together. Curdon Mill is on a sharp right-hand bend before you reach Stogumber.

CURDON MILL
Owners: Daphne & Richard Criddle
Lower Vellow, Stogumber
Taunton
Somerset TA4 4LS, England
Tel: (01984) 656522, Fax: (01984) 656197
E-mail: curdonmill@compuserve.com
www.karenbrown.com/england/curdonmill.html
6 rooms
£30–£55 per person, dinner £19.50–£24
Open all year
Credit cards: all major
Children over 8

The food at The Angel Inn is outstanding and, fortunately for visitors to this pretty part of Suffolk, guests may lodge as well as dine here. When Peter Smith and Richard Wright purchased the inn in 1985, it was in a sorry state, but now its complete refurbishment has transformed it into a building with lots of charm and old-world ambiance. Guests eating in the bar (best advised to avoid the crush by arriving early or just before last orders at 9 pm) make their selection from the menu hung on the old red-brick wall above the fireplace and then settle down at one of the tables grouped under the low, beamed ceiling. Those who prefer a quieter atmosphere and the security of a reservation elect to pay the £1.50 per person cover charge to reserve a table in the dramatic 16th century hall with its lofty rafters. Tables are laid with linen and soft lighting adds a romantic mood. Wherever you dine you have the identical choice of tempting fare. Bedrooms are pleasantly furnished and have a light, airy decor. This unspoilt region of quiet countryside offers lots of sightseeing, such as the nearby valley of the River Stour, Dedham, and Flatford Mill, all made famous by John Constable's paintings. *Directions:* Take the A134 Sudbury road from Colchester for 5 miles to Nayland, then turn right for the 2-mile drive to Stoke by Nayland.

THE ANGEL INN
Owners: Richard Wright & Peter Smith
Stoke by Nayland
Colchester
Essex CO6 4SA, England
Tel: (01206) 263245, Fax: (01206) 263373
www.karenbrown.com/england/theangelinn.html
6 rooms
£30.50–£32.50 per person, dinner £15–£20
Closed Christmas
Credit cards: all major
Children over 10

Just a few minutes' walk from town, this square, three-story building with rich salmon-colored façade and white trim stands out amongst the many row houses offering bed and breakfast accommodation. Although we only just discovered the delightful, family-run Caterham House Hotel, it has existed under the same proprietorship for 25 years and the register boasts a majority of loyal returning guests. With the owners being originally from France, this hotel has a charming, subtly French influence both in its decor and ambiance. Soft tones of yellow and mauve dominate the color scheme and creative touches such as attractive stenciling, interesting art, and a beautiful quilt hung as a headboard make each room refreshing and unique. Off the entry there is a welcoming sitting room with full bar and outside terrace for guests to enjoy. To accommodate the ten guestrooms in the main building, Dominique and Olive cleverly took down the shared wall of two adjoining buildings, so when you climb the interior stairs it seems almost an illusion as an apparently mirrored staircase rises up to meet the other. Ten years ago they also renovated a neighboring cottage to house two additional rooms. Although there is no restaurant, Dominique tailors breakfast to whatever guests want, be it traditional English with eggs and sausage or French with croissants and coffee. *Directions:* Turn left at the American Fountain coming from the town center, and right coming from the train station, into Rother Street. The Caterham House Hotel is on the left just past the police station.

*CATERHAM HOUSE HOTEL   **New***
Owners: Olive & Dominique Maury
58/59 Rother Street
Stratford-upon-Avon
Warwickshire CV37 6LT, England
Tel: (01789) 267309, Fax: (01789) 414836
12 rooms
£36–£41 per person
Open all year, Credit cards: MC, VS
Children welcome

One of the joys of staying in Sydling St. Nicholas is wandering along the rushing little stream admiring the idyllically pretty thatched cottages and houses that make up this totally unspoilt Dorset village. Upper Mill, once a prosperous miller's home, has been completely restored by Sally and Colin Anderson. Guests have a comfortable sitting room for relaxing in the evening and enjoy breakfast in the conservatory looking over the garden out to the sheep grazing on Cowdown Hill. Upstairs, the pretty bedrooms consist of a large double-bedded room with small shower room and a twin-bedded room with adjacent spacious bathroom. There are three very good pubs that serve dinner in the nearby village of Cerne Abbas. Sally (a former tour guide) is a friendly hostess and thoroughly enjoys helping guests decide what to see and where to go, whether it be to unspoilt beaches, gorgeous gardens, or stately homes or just driving through the lovely Dorset villages. *Directions:* From Dorchester take the A37 towards Yeovil. After about 3 miles pass through Grimstone and just beyond the village turn right for Sydling St. Nicholas. Drive 4 miles up the valley into the village and Upper Mill is the tall house on the right just past The Greyhound pub.

UPPER MILL
Owners: Sally & Colin Anderson
Sydling St. Nicholas
Dorchester
Dorset DT2 9PD, England
Tel & fax: (01300) 341230
2 rooms, 1 en suite
£26 per person
Closed Christmas
Credit cards: none
Children over 12
No-smoking house

Thomas Luny, the marine artist, had this home built in 1792 in the center of Teignmouth, just a short walk through narrow streets from the sheltered harbor which has a long history as a fishing and ship-building center. Now this handsome house is home to Alison and John Allan and their two children. All the rooms have an en-suite bathroom, a television, mineral water, and a lovely old sea chest. Each is decorated in a contrasting style: Chinese enjoys a peach-and-green decor and painted Oriental furniture; Clairmont is pretty in green and yellow; Luny is autumnal in beige and brown; and Bitton contemporary with its impressive four-poster bed. A scrumptious breakfast is the only meal served but there is no shortage of eating places a few minutes' walk or a short drive away. Follow the narrow streets of old Teignmouth to the working harbor and along to the Victorian section of town with its long sandy beach, cheerful pier, and esplanade popular with the bucket-and-spade brigade. Just across the estuary lies Shaldon where every Wednesday, from May to September, residents dress in 18th-century costume. *Directions:* From Exeter take the A380 towards Torquay for 3 miles to the B3192 to Teignmouth. Turn left at the traffic lights at the bottom of the hill, then turn immediately right at next set of traffic lights, signposted Quays, and immediately left into Teign Street. Thomas Luny House is on your right.

THOMAS LUNY HOUSE
Owners: Alison & John Allan
Teign Street
Teignmouth
Devon TQ14 8EG, England
Tel: (01626) 772976, Fax: none
www.karenbrown.com/england/thomasluny.html
4 rooms
£25–£35 per person
Open all year
Credit cards: MC, VS
Children over 12

Dale Head Hall occupies a stunning, isolated position on the shores of Thirlmere, one of Cumbria's quietest, most pastoral lakes, and provides the perfect base for exploring the entire Lake District. Bedrooms at the front of the hotel offer gorgeous lake views while the delightful rooms at the back in the old part of the house are low-ceilinged with old latch doors and beams. One of the back bedrooms has a small cradle room snug above the inglenook fireplace. (One of the lake-view bedrooms is handily located on the ground floor.) Superior rooms are rented only on a dinner, bed, and breakfast basis. Much of the lovely oak furniture found throughout the hotel is the handiwork of personable Alan Lowe who joins his wife Shirley, daughter Caroline, and son-in-law Hans in making certain that guests are well taken care of and well fed. The cottagey dining room is in the oldest part of the house. Walks from the hotel range from a stroll around the lake to challenging hikes up the nearby fells. For a week's stay, Dale Head Hall has several delightful apartments in the adjacent stables. *Directions:* Leave the M6 at junction 40 and take the A66 towards Keswick then the B5322 signposted Windermere to join the A591 which you take in the direction of Windermere for ½ mile. The entrance to Dale Head Hall is on your right.

DALE HEAD HALL
Owners: Shirley & Alan Lowe
Caroline & Hans Bonkenburg
Lake Thirlmere, Keswick
Cumbria CA12 4TN, England
Tel: (017687) 72478, Fax: (017687) 71070
E-mail: holiday@dale-head-hall.co.uk
www.karenbrown.com/ews/daleheadhall.html
9 rooms, 5 apartments
£42.50–£50 per person, dinner £27.50
Superior room £80–£87.50 per person*
*Dinner, bed, & breakfast
Open Feb to Dec, Credit cards: all major
Children welcome

Claiming the honor of being King Arthur's legendary birthplace, the ruins of Tintagel Castle cling to a wild headland exposed to the coastal winds. It's a place of myths that attracts visitors who come to soak up its fanciful past and enjoy its rugged scenery. While the village of Tintagel is a touristy spot, just a mile away lies the quiet hamlet of Trenale, a cluster of cottages, and the delightful Trebrea Lodge. Behind the impressive, tall Georgian façade lies a much older building of cozy, comfortable rooms. Upstairs, the drawing room is full of splendid antiques but you will probably find yourself downstairs toasting your toes by the fire enveloped by a large armchair, enjoying drinks and coffee after one of Sean's delicious award-winning dinners in the paneled dining room with its views across stone-walled fields to the distant sea. We particularly enjoyed our room (4) furnished, as are all the rooms, with lovely antiques and enjoying a large bathroom; the four-poster room (1) with its ornately carved Victorian four-poster bed; and room 5, a delightful twin-bedded room with its view to the distant ocean. A tempting array of hot breakfast dishes is placed on the buffet for guests to help themselves. Walkers enjoy spectacular cliff-top walks along rugged headlands. To the north lies Clovelly. *Directions:* From Tintagel take the road towards Boscastle and at the edge of Tintagel turn right at the contemporary-style Roman Catholic church. Turn right at the top of the lane and Trebrea Lodge is on your left.

TREBREA LODGE
Owners: John Charlick & Sean Devlin
Trenale, Tintagel
Cornwall PL34 0HR, England
Tel: (01840) 770410, Fax: (01840) 770092
www.karenbrown.com/england/trebrealodge.html
7 rooms
£42–£47 per person, dinner £23
Open mid-Feb to mid-Dec
Credit cards: all major
Children over 12

Marjorie and Euan Aitken's home is a picture-book thatched cottage in an idyllically quiet Oxfordshire village (yet it's only a 45-minute drive to Heathrow airport), nestled beside a duck pond with a rowboat moored beneath overhanging willows. When the Aitkens restored the cottage, they preserved all the lovely old features they uncovered: an old range and copper boiler, beams with the carpenter's identification marks, and a pump. Every room is furnished with antiques and decorated with collections of bric-a-brac and country bygones. Across the farmyard the timbered barn has been converted to provide immaculate guestrooms with modern showers, televisions, exposed beams, and displays of Marjorie's collections. I particularly enjoyed Mary Queen of Scots (the rooms are named after royals), with its corridor hung with farm implements, a Cumberland quilt decorating the bedroom wall, and its choirboy-vestments cupboard used as a closet. Breakfast is the only meal served in the country-pine breakfast room. The milking shed next door, which enjoys a private entrance and a serene setting overlooking the neighboring stream, has been converted into two more en-suite ground-floor bedrooms with wheelchair access. Blenheim Palace and Oxford colleges are less than half an hour away. Nearby Waddesden Manor, the ancestral Rothschild home, has a spectacular art collection. *Directions:* Exit the M40 at junction 6 and take the B4009 to Chinnor where you turn left on the B4445 towards Thame. After 2 miles turn right to Towersey, right at the crossroads, and the farm is on your left at the end of the village.

UPPER GREEN FARM
Owners: Marjorie & Euan Aitken
Manor Road, Towersey
Oxfordshire OX9 3QR, England
Tel: (01844) 212496, Fax: (01844) 260399
E-mail: bandb@ugfarm.free-online.co.uk
www.karenbrown.com/england/uppergreenfarm.html
10 rooms
£25–£32.50 per person
Closed Christmas & New Year, Credit cards: none
Children over 13, No-smoking house

Jane and Steven Epperson lived in both America and England (he's American, she's English) before deciding to settle in Cornwall, where they bought Anchorage House as the shell of an impressive home and finished it off in a grand Georgian style. Furnished throughout in antiques, the home has the advantage of having a traditional feel accompanied by all the luxurious modern conveniences of king- or queen-sized beds, satellite television, individually controlled central heating, power showers, and generous-sized baths. Guests often relax in the conservatory where breakfast is taken overlooking the garden and lap pool. Jane is happy to offer the occasional dinner round the antique dining-room table or direct guests to the excellent pubs and restaurants within a few minutes' walk or drive. Anchorage House's location on a quiet cul-de-sac just off the A390 makes it ideal for those who want to avoid navigating narrow Cornish lanes to reach their accommodation and also means that it is handily placed for making driving forays to places as near as the Lost Gardens of Helligan (10 minutes' drive) and as far away as Land's End and St. Michael's Mount (1 hour's drive). *Directions:* Anchorage House is on the A390, 1 mile west of St. Blazey, 2 miles east of St. Austell. Opposite the St. Austell Garden Center turn into a small lane signposted Tregrehan and then immediately left into a private driveway leading to Anchorage House.

ANCHORAGE HOUSE
Owners: Jane & Steven Epperson
Nettles Corner, Tregrehan, St. Austell
Cornwall PL25 3RH, England
Tel: (01726) 814071, Fax: none
3 rooms
£30–£34 per person, dinner £25
Open all year
Credit cards: MC, VS
Children over 16
No-smoking house
Wolsey Lodge

Pat and Richard Mason transformed a tumbledown cottage and barn in an overgrown field by a stream into a delightful home facing a lake in an idyllic 6-acre garden complete with stream and many unusual plants and shrubs. The house is just as attractive inside as out. Sofas are drawn up around the wood-burning stove in the beamed sitting room. In addition to a double room on the ground floor the accommodation consists of two further, very nicely furnished bedrooms upstairs. All rooms have extremely powerful showers in newly equipped shower rooms. During the warm summer months, evening barbecues may be served on the terrace or in the conservatory (with prior notice). There are many alternative eating places locally. One of Patsy's suggested day trips takes in The National Rose collection at Mottisfont Abbey, Hilliers Arboretum, and finally Broadlands, the home of the late Lord Mountbatten. Salisbury, Winchester, and Stonehenge are all 15 miles distant. Other services include airport collection from Heathrow and Gatwick with car hire delivered to Malt Cottage and trout fishing on one of the many local water—including the famous River Test. *Directions:* From the A303, at Andover, take the A3057 (Stockbridge road) and turn first right, signposted for Upper Clatford. Take the first left, go right at the T-junction, and turn right opposite the Crook and Shears pub into a little lane which leads to Malt Cottage.

MALT COTTAGE
Owners: Patsy & Richard Mason
Upper Clatford
Andover
Hampshire SP11 7QL, England
Tel: (01264) 323469, Fax: (01264) 334100
E-mail: maltcottage.accommodation@virgin.net
www.karenbrown.com/england/maltcottage.html
3 rooms, 1 en suite
£25–£30 per person, dinner £15
Closed Christmas & New Year, Credit cards: none
Children welcome, No-smoking house

Standing on the corner of St. John's Hill, a charming little square on the edge of the very attractive little town of Wareham, Gold Court House was built in 1762 on the foundations of a 13th-century cottage where the local goldsmith lived. Now it is the spacious, lovely home of Anthea and Michael Hipwell and, fortunately for guests, they continue to offer the same hospitable welcome (along with a tail-wagging greeting from Cedar the Labrador) as they did for over 15 years at The Old Vicarage in Affpuddle. All the spacious, well-decorated bedrooms overlook the lovely walled garden. Two are found up the main staircase, while the third has a private entry off the garden. Breakfast is the only meal served but Anthea offers advice on pubs and restaurants to walk to for dinner. Likewise, Anthea helps guests plan their exploration of Hardy country or visits to the haunts of Lawrence of Arabia. The Dorset coast (Lulworth Cove, Dirdle Door, and Ringstead Bay) is close at hand. Nearby are the historic towns of Dorchester, Sherbourne, and Poole, with lots to see and good shopping. *Directions:* Wareham is on the A351 between Poole and Swanage. Cross the River Piddle and go down North Street into South Street. As you see the River Frome in front of you, turn left into St. John's Hill. Gold Court House is on the corner.

GOLD COURT HOUSE
Owners: Anthea & Michael Hipwell
St. John's Hill
Wareham
Dorset BH20 4LZ, England
Tel & fax: (01929) 553320
3 rooms
£22.50–£25 per person, dinner £11(winter only)
Closed Christmas to New Year
Credit cards: none
Children over 10
No-smoking house

Corrie has the most spectacular Lake District location—just a couple of fields separate it from Ullswater with the fells rising sharply from the far shore. For many years this was Eileen Pattinson's holiday home, a converted barn complex extended to maximize and capture the spectacular views. Now Eileen and her partner Charles run Corrie on traditional house party lines, sharing their lovely home with guests. The two principal bedrooms are very spacious and the smaller single room has its shower room across the hall. The garden is a delight and includes a tennis court. Guests often wander across the fields to the lake where you can swim, though the water is pretty cold. Being just a ten-minute drive from the motorway, it's an ideal spot to break your journey to or from Scotland, but do extend your stay beyond one night as the area has much to recommend it besides the utter peace and quiet that you encounter at Corrie. For the energetic, the Lakeland fells offer endless opportunities ranging from strolls to serious hikes, while touring by car presents gorgeous lake and mountain vistas. *Directions:* Leave the M6 at junction 40, taking the A66 towards Keswick for ½ mile to the large roundabout. Turn left for Ullswater on the A592 and on reaching the lake, turn right, signposted Windermere, on a road tracing the lake. Continue for 2 miles, past the Brackenrigg Hotel, down to the bottom of the hill. The entrance to Corrie is opposite a junction and telephone box.

CORRIE
Owners: Eileen Pattinson & Charles Pope
Watermillock, Penrith
Cumbria CA11 0JH, England
Tel & fax: (017684) 86582
www.karenbrown.com/england/corrie.html
3 rooms, 2 en suite
£41 per person, dinner £25
Open Apr to mid-Dec
Credit cards: none
Children over 10
No-smoking house

Beryl, a Gothic revival mansion on 13 acres of grounds just a mile from Wells Cathedral, is a grand house full of lovely antiques and home to Holly and Eddie Nowell and their family—a home they enjoy sharing with their guests. The measure of their success is the large number of returning guests who bring their family, friends, and even dogs (provided that they are compatible with the resident chocolate Labs). Lovers of elegant antiques will delight in those found in every nook and cranny of the house—Eddie is a well-known antique dealer. All the bedrooms have special features. We loved our attic room, Summer, all pretty in pink and white with daisies on the wallpaper and bedcovers. Next door, Spring has an elegantly draped four-poster bed to leap (literally) into. Principal bedrooms are larger and grander—choose Winston if you have a passion for grand, old-fashioned, climb-into bathtubs, Butterfly if you enjoy space and want to wake up with Wells Cathedral framed in the enormous bay window. Wells is England's smallest city, with the most glorious cathedral. *Directions:* Leave or approach Wells on the B3139 in the direction of The Horrington's. Turn into Hawkers Lane (not Beryl Lane) opposite the BP garage. Drive to the top of the lane and continue straight into Beryl's driveway.

BERYL
Owners: Holly & Eddie Nowell
Hawkers Lane
Wells
Somerset BA5 3JP, England
Tel: (01749) 678738, Fax: (01749) 670508
www.karenbrown.com/england/beryl.html
7 rooms
£32.50–£47.50 per person, dinner £20
Closed Christmas
Credit cards: MC, VS
Children welcome
Wolsey Lodge

The Citadel sits like a mighty fortress on a knoll overlooking verdant countryside. As soon as you cross the threshold, you realize this is not a "castle" of drafty halls and stone chambers, but a lovely home built to a fanciful design. A spacious sitting room occupies one of the turrets and leads to the large billiard room. Sylvia and her husband, Beverley, often join guests for sherry before dinner and then guests dine together round the long dining-room table. You are welcome to bring your own wine. Up the broad staircase, two of the bedrooms occupy turrets. Each has an adjacent Victorian-style bathroom with center-stage claw-foot tub. A twin-bedded room has an en-suite shower room. The adjacent golf club is a popular venue, but the real magic of the area lies in a visit to Hawkstone Park where you follow an intricate network of pathways through woodlands and across a narrow log bridge to high cliffs, a ruined castle, mystical grotto, and giant obelisk. The Ironbridge Gorge Museums, Shrewsbury, and Chester are within an hour's drive. *Directions:* From Shrewsbury, take the A49 (north) for 12 miles, turn right for Hodnet and Weston-under-Redcastle, and The Citadel is on your right, a quarter of a mile after leaving Weston-under-Redcastle (before Hawkstone Park).

THE CITADEL
Owners: Sylvia & Beverley Griffiths
Weston-under-Redcastle
Shrewsbury
Shropshire SY4 5JY, England
Tel & fax: (01630) 685204
3 rooms, 1 en suite
£37.50–£40 per person, dinner £16–£20
Open Apr to Oct
Credit cards: none
Children over 12
No-smoking house
Wolsey Lodge

Built in 1692, Dearnford Hall has been the Bebbington family home for three generations. Now that the children have grown up and flown the nest, Jane enjoys looking after her guests while her husband Chas is busy running their 500-acre arable farm. The atmosphere is relaxed and friendly, the decor is delightful, and the large bedrooms with their sparkling modern bathrooms rival those of elegant country house hotels. After a restful night's sleep and a hearty English breakfast served by the fire in the dining room, you can explore Chester, perfect for browsing in antique stores, or Shrewsbury, and follow in the steps of Brother Cadfael, the medieval sleuthing monk. Snowdonia, The Potteries, Ironbridge, and a wealth of National Trust houses, castles, and gardens are all within easy reach. Jane recommends a variety of excellent restaurants or pubs for an evening meal. Feel free to bring your own tipple home and relax by a log fire to round off your day. There is a lovely walk through the fields to the 15-acre spring-fed trout lake—Molly, their flat-coat retriever, will be happy to escort you. Those keen to pursue the art of fly-fishing can fish from bank or boat. Should you wish to improve your casting techniques, lessons and rods can be arranged. *Directions:* From Whitchurch bypass take the B5476 towards Tilstock and Wem for half a mile and Dearnford Hall is the second farm on the left-hand side.

DEARNFORD HALL
Owners: Jane & Chas Bebbington
Whitchurch,
Shropshire SY13 3JJ, England
Tel: (01948) 662319, Fax: (01948) 666670
E-mail: dearnford_hall@yahoo.com
www.karenbrown.com/england/dearnford.html
2 rooms
£38–£50 per person
Closed Christmas
Credit cards: none
Children over 15, No-smoking house

Willersey's duck pond sits on the village green overlooked by golden-stone cottages. The lane that runs beside the pub leads to The Old Rectory, sitting in a spacious garden with the 11th-century village church as its closest neighbor. The mulberry tree in the garden is reputed to have been planted in the reign of Queen Elizabeth I and still provides fruit for breakfast. Bedrooms in The Old Rectory come in all shapes and sizes, from a snug attic room where bathrobes are provided for padding across the hall to grander en-suite rooms with four-poster beds. For a family or two couples traveling together, the Bridle and Saddle rooms in the coach house have intercommunicating doors. Guestrooms are well equipped with excellent firm beds, hairdryers, and quality toiletries. Individual tables are set for breakfast. In the evening guests usually stroll down to the Bell Inn for dinner (flashlights are provided for guiding your way home). If you are looking to rent an adorable, old-world, two-bedroom cottage, consider Church End Cottage opposite The Old Rectory, overlooking the churchyard and Cotswold escarpment. The Old Rectory is a perfect base for touring the Cotswolds. A delightful day trip takes you farther afield to Stratford-upon-Avon and Warwick Castle. *Directions:* From Broadway take the B4632 towards Stratford-upon-Avon for 1½ miles to Willersey. Turn right into Church Street at the Bell and The Old Rectory is at the end of the lane.

THE OLD RECTORY
Owners: Liz & Chris Beauvoisin
Church Street
Willersey, nr Broadway
Gloucestershire WR12 7PN, England
Tel: (01386) 853729, Fax: (01386) 858061
E-mail: beauvoisin@btinternet.com
www.karenbrown.com/england/theoldrectorywillersey.html
8 rooms, 6 en suite, 1 cottage
£35–£55 per person
Closed Christmas
Credit cards: all major
Children over 8, No-smoking house

One of the attractions for garden lovers staying at Tavern House is that Westonbirt Arboretum with its 600 acres of trees is just down the road. Although the house sits right beside the A433, there is no noise problem—thick walls and double glazing do the job in the daytime and the road is quiet at night. Breakfast is the only meal served at the cottagey little tables and chairs in the dining room and guests often go to the nearby village of Sherston to the Rattlebone Inn for dinner. A log fire is lit in the guests' sitting room on cool evenings. All of the bedrooms are very private as each of the four rooms has its own narrow little staircase. Room 1 is especially spacious with its high, beamed ceiling rising to the rafters, a small dressing room (ideal for parking large cases), and a bathroom large enough to accommodate a bath and separate shower. Janet and Tim used to own a large hotel in Salcombe and they have applied the same professional standards to their bed and breakfast venture. Sightseeing within a 25-mile radius includes the little market town of Chipping Sodbury; Badminton House, a superb Palladian mansion; the market town of Cirencester; Bath and Cheltenham with their Regency houses; Slimbridge Wildfowl Trust; and Berkeley Castle. *Directions:* Leave the M4 at junction 18, take the A46 (Stroud, Cirencester) to the A433 towards Tetbury. Tavern House is on your right 1 mile before Westonbirt Arboretum. Park in the lane and ring the front door bell, or use the outdoor phone.

TAVERN HOUSE
Owners: Janet & Tim Tremellen
Willesley, near Tetbury
Gloucestershire GL8 8QU, England
Tel: (01666) 880444, Fax: (01666) 880254
www.karenbrown.com/england/tavernhouse.html
4 rooms
£31.50–£34.50 per person
Open all year
Credit cards: MC, VS
Children over 10

Stratford-upon-Avon is a Mecca for visitors who come for everything associated with Shakespeare: the performances of his plays, the town's Tudor buildings, Anne Hathaway's cottage, and Mary Arden's house. Just across the garden from Mary Arden's house you find Pear Tree Cottage, home to Margaret and Ted Mander for almost forty years, a home that has been sympathetically extended to provide seven en-suite bedrooms for guests. All the rooms are delightful, though I particularly enjoyed those in the old cottage simply because they have an especially old-world feeling. Guests have an attractive small sitting room and breakfast room with little tables and chairs set in front of a dresser displaying decorative blue-and-white plates. Two modern kitchens are available for guests to prepare their picnics or suppers and there is a washing machine for those who need to do laundry. Margaret and Ted really look after guests, providing them with an excellent map of Stratford that highlights all the things to see and, most importantly, indicates where to conveniently park your car when sightseeing or going to the theater (they can help guests to obtain tickets). Another map outlines a day tour through Cotswold villages, highlighting all the gardens, villages, houses and pubs. *Directions:* From Stratford-upon-Avon take the A3400 signposted for Henley-in-Arden for 2½ miles. Turn left to Wilmcote and Pear Tree Cottage is in the center of the village.

PEAR TREE COTTAGE
Owners: Margaret & Ted Mander
Church Road, Wilmcote
Stratford-upon-Avon
Warwickshire CV37 9UX, England
Tel: (01789) 205889, Fax: (01789) 262862
www.karenbrown.com/england/peartreecottageage.html
7 rooms
£24–£26 per person
Open Feb to Dec
Credit cards: none
Children over 3, No-smoking house

Nestled beside the baby River Isbourne on a quiet county lane just a few yards from the main street of the delightfully pretty Cotswold village of Winchcombe, Isbourne Manor House dates back to Elizabethan times, with extensive Georgian additions. From the moment you enter, you will be delighted by the attractive decor and warmth of hospitality offered by Felicity and David King. The elegant drawing room with its wood-burning fire is exclusively for guests' use. Breakfast is the only meal served in the dining room, but the Kings provide an extensive list of suggested eating places in the area. Splurge and request The Sudeley Room, well worth the few additional pounds to enjoy its elegant queen-sized four-poster bed swathed with peach-colored draperies. Langley is a most attractive double-bedded room decorated in shades of cream. Under the steeply sloping eaves of the Elizabethan portion of the house you find the snug quarters offered by Beesmore whose window serves as the door onto a large rooftop terrace. Beesmore's bathroom is down the hall. Walk to nearby Sudeley Castle, more of a stately home than a traditional castle, then set out on a day-long tour of Cotswold villages with Bourton-on-the-Water, Stow-on-the-Wold, Chipping Campden, and Broadway being popular destinations. *Directions:* Winchcombe is on the B4632 between Cheltenham and Broadway. Turn into Castle Street (in the center of the village) and Isbourne Manor House is on the left just before the little bridge.

ISBOURNE MANOR HOUSE
Owners: Felicity & David King
Castle Street, Winchcombe
Gloucestershire GL54 6JA, England
Tel & fax: (01242) 602281
www.karenbrown.com/england/isbournemanorhouse.html
3 rooms, 2 en suite
£27.50–£35 per person
Open all year
Credit cards: none
Children over 10, No-smoking house

Sudeley Lodge, built in 1760 as a grand home on the Sudeley Castle estate, sits high on a hill overlooking rolling countryside beyond its acres of gorgeous gardens. Jim grew up here and when his parents found the house too big for them, they divided it into two with Jim, Susie, and their family having the Westward wing. Susie welcomes guests with tea and cake, encouraging them to make themselves at home in the drawing room, wander round the gardens, and walk on the farm. Upstairs, the spacious bedrooms have lovely views across the garden to the countryside. Susie loves to cook and candlelit dinners are sometimes available. There is no shortage of excellent places to eat both in nearby Winchcombe and the surrounding villages. Just down the road is Sudeley Castle with its parklike setting, magnificent medieval exterior, and largely Victorianized interior. This is an ideal spot for exploring a plethora of Cotswold villages such as Broadway, Snowshill, Chipping Campden, Lower Slaughter, and Stow-on-the-Wold. *Directions:* Winchcombe is on the B4632 between Cheltenham and Broadway. Turn into Castle Street (in the center of the village) and proceed up the hill. Pass the farm buildings on the right and turn right signed Sudeley Lodge. Pass two cottages on the way to the house.

WESTWARD AT SUDELEY LODGE
Owners: Susie & Jim Wilson
Winchcombe
Gloucestershire GL54 5JB, England
Tel & fax: (01242) 604372
E-mail: westward@aol.com
3 rooms
£35–£42.50 per person, dinner £22.50
Closed Christmas & New Year
Credit cards: MC, VS
Children over 12

Bed & Breakfast Descriptions   151

Just beside the cathedral in a maze of little streets in the oldest part of Winchester, you can find comfortable accommodation at The Saint George and, across the road, under the same ownership, at The Wykeham Arms. The Saint George was converted from two tiny row houses and has the quaint attraction of a post office and shop just off the parlor. I love its immaculate rooms—up the narrow staircase there are four large bedrooms, with absolutely everything from a sumptuous bathroom to a fax or modem point beside the desk, and a snug single. If you are looking for more spacious accommodation, settle down for several days in the Old College Bakehouse, a little cottage in the garden, with its large sitting room and bathroom downstairs and upstairs a bedroom with tall, arched, leaded windows opening up to rooftop views. The Wykeham Arms, with newly refurbished bedrooms, is an extraordinary Victorian pub where over 600 pictures decorate the walls, 1,000 tankards hang from beams, walls, and windows, and Winchester memorabilia abounds. Its pub menu is posted on the board in the bar, and offers choices ranging from elaborate to tasty traditional fare. Quieter tables can be reserved in the Bishop's Bar or the Watchmaker's Room. *Directions:* Winchester is between junctions 9 and 10 on the M3. The Saint George and The Wykeham Arms are located near the cathedral. Tim will send you a map so that you can navigate your car through the pedestrian zone to the pub's car park.

THE SAINT GEORGE & THE WYKEHAM ARMS
Manager: Tim Manktelo Gray
King's Gate
Winchester SO23 9PD, England
Tel: (01962) 853834, Fax: (01962) 854411
www.karenbrown.com/england/wykehamarms.html
12 rooms
£41–£60 per person, dinner £20 (average)
Closed Christmas
Credit cards: all major
Children over 14

Hawksmoor Guest House appears no different from the many other guesthouses on these well-traveled Lake District roads until one enters, sees, and appreciates the apple-pie-order of Barbara and Bob Tyson's home. The decor is not fancy or pretentious, for this is not an expensive country house hotel, but it is well maintained: Bob boasts, "If it's broken or damaged today, it will be fixed by tomorrow." The dining room is delightfully set with pink tablecloths covered with delicate lace and laid with silver service. Barbara is happy for guests to eat in or out, always willing to provide a traditional English three-course dinner. Guests have a small comfortable lounge at their disposal. The bedrooms are smallish but each is decorated with pretty flowered wallpaper with matching curtains and bedspreads, and all have en-suite bathrooms. Robert is an expert on the Lake District and even manages to suggest a sight or two to the hurried traveler who is dashing through this lovely part of England and using it as a one-night stop on the road between London and Edinburgh. He has found that these rushed travelers often return for a stay of several days. Windermere is in the heart of the busy southern Lake District, easily accessible from the M6. *Directions:* Windermere is just off the A591 Ambleside to Kendal road. Drive along New Road and look for Hawksmoor on the right just after the clock tower.

HAWKSMOOR GUEST HOUSE
Owners: Barbara & Bob Tyson
Lake Road
Windermere
Cumbria LA23 2EQ, England
Tel: (015394) 42110, Fax: none
www.karenbrown.com/england/hawksmoorguesthouse.html
10 rooms
£27–£32 per person, dinner £12.50
Open Feb to Nov
Credit cards: MC, VS
Children over 6

Just 5 miles from the Georgian splendors of Bath, Burghope Manor is the 13th-century home of Liz and John Denning. Much of the present house dates from Tudor times and Burghope has strong associations with Henry VIII's prelate Archbishop Cranmer. Liz is a vivacious person who loves meeting people from all walks of life and all over the world and enjoys sharing her lovely home with them. Guests are encouraged to make themselves at home in the large pink drawing room, though they often prefer the cozier confines of the morning room. Upstairs, the spacious, lovely bedrooms, all equipped with color TV and tea- and coffee-making facilities, are each accompanied by an en-suite bathroom with bath and shower. For dinner, guests stroll into Winsley village to dine at the Seven Stars pub or Nightingales restaurant. If you are planning on staying a week or more, consider renting the Dower House, a luxurious three-bed three-bath home sitting in the grounds. There are enough activities in Bath and nearby Bradford on Avon, to occupy a week. *Directions:* From Bath take the A36 towards Warminster for 5 miles and turn left on the B3108 signposted Winsley and Bradford on Avon. Follow the road up the hill to Winsley, at the start of the bypass take the first right into the village, then at the mini crossroads turn left. The manor's front gates are at the top of the lane.

BURGHOPE MANOR
Owners: Liz & John Denning
Winsley
Bradford on Avon
Wiltshire BA15 LA, England
Tel: (01225) 723557, Fax: (01225) 723113
E-mail: info@burghopemanor.co.uk
www.karenbrown.com/england/burghopemanor.html
8 rooms
£40–£45 per person
Closed Christmas & New Year
Credit cards: all major
Children over 10, No-smoking house

The Old Wharf's idyllic setting provides an entrancing first impression. A lane leading off the main highway wends its way down to a delightful small building hugging the edge of a tiny canal. Nearby, cows graze peacefully in meadows that stretch as far as the eye can see. The enclosed front patio is ablaze with a riot of color: a luxuriant cottage garden of colorful flowers, beautifully manicured yet artfully exuberant. The side of the house that opens onto the meandering stream is laced with climbing white roses. The spell of the initial impression remains unbroken when you go inside. Moira and David have taken an old warehouse and converted it into their home, incorporating an outstanding small bed and breakfast. The decor throughout is fresh and airy and extremely pretty. Moira has managed to cleverly combine lovely pastel fabrics with natural-wood-finish antiques to achieve a very pretty country look. Primrose has a small double-bedded bedroom and a snug sitting room with tall windows opening up to views of the river and fields. Breakfast is the only meal served. Within easy reach are the towns of the Sussex coast, Petworth House, and Arundel Castle. *Directions:* From Billingshurst take the A272 towards Petworth, cross the canal and river, and The Old Wharf is 50 yards after the river on the left.

THE OLD WHARF
Owners: Moira & David Mitchell
Wisborough Green
Billingshurst
Sussex RH14 0JG, England
Tel & fax: (01403) 784096
3 rooms
£30–£40 per person
Closed Dec 15 to Jan 6
Credit cards: all major
Children over 12
No-smoking house

Woodstock huddles by the gates of Blenheim Palace, the home of the 11th Duke of Marlborough and birthplace of Sir Winston Churchill. Holmwood offers the ideal location for exploring the Cotswolds, touring Blenheim with its vast grounds, and visiting the nearby university city of Oxford, yet it is only a 1½-hour drive from London. This golden-Cotswold-stone Queen-Anne house sitting on the main village street (not the main traffic street) proudly displays the date 1710. Christina and her Italian husband Roberto have been in the hospitality industry for many years and certainly know how to please their guests. With just two deluxe suites, each occupying a complete level of the house, Holmwood offers spacious accommodations. On the first floor (second in America) you enter a sitting room with a writing desk, television, and two comfortable chairs. This leads to a large, beamed bedroom with two big windows with window seats overlooking the village street and a bed that can be made up as twins or a king. The luxurious bathroom has both a shower and a tub and a door which opens onto an outside staircase leading into the garden. Above this sits an equally lovely queen-bedded suite. *Directions:* High Street is off Oxford Street, which is the A44 Oxford to Stratford-upon-Avon road. Park in front of Holmwood to unload your suitcases and Christina or Roberto will direct you to parking.

HOLMWOOD
Owners: Christina & Roberto Gramellini
6 High Street
Woodstock
Oxfordshire OX20 1TF, England
Tel: (01993) 812266, Fax: (01993) 813233
E-mail: christina@holm-wood.demon.co.uk
www.karenbrown.com/england/holmwood.html
2 rooms
£37.50–£40 per person
Closed Jan
Credit cards: none
Children over 12, No-smoking house

This unusual, late-Victorian house has been lovingly restored by its resident owners, Sue and Stan Long. Sue and Stan are locals with a warm appreciation of their historic hometown. The guest sitting room's small bar also doubles as the reception and guests sit next to a Laurel and Hardy sculpture to watch a short video outlining York's major sights. Up the staircase, each of the six bedrooms contains an antique four-poster bed. Room 2 has a delightful, modern, Victorian-style bathroom and the Longs plan to convert several other more dated bathrooms to this style. Breakfast is the only meal served in the little pink dining room whose window is noted for being one of the few in York that is still charged a light tax. After a hearty breakfast it's time to get acquainted with the many delights of York, see the magnificent Minster, explore the Viking City of Jorvik, and experience times past in the Castle Museum. Guests often enjoy interesting stories in the evening when they join a guide on a ghost walk through the historic streets of this ancient city. *Directions:* Leave the A64 (which forms the southern part of the York Outer Ring Road) at the A1036, in the direction of York city center (signposted York West). Pass the racecourse on your right and just after the Mount Royal Hotel (also on the right) take the second turn right on Scarcroft Road and first right into Scarcroft Hill. Grasmead House is on the corner of Scarcroft Hill and Scarcroft Road, overlooking the park. Parking is on the street.

GRASMEAD HOUSE
Owners: Sue & Stan Long
1 Scarcroft Hill
York YO2 1DF, England
Tel & fax: (01904) 629996
E-mail: stansue@grasmeadhouse.freeserve.co.uk
6 rooms
£35–£37.50 per person
Open all year
Credit cards: MC, VS
Children welcome

Located on a quiet side street just a 15-minute walk from the heart of historic York, Hobbits is a delightful bed and breakfast. This turn-of-the-century home still retains its spacious downstairs rooms, mahogany staircase, and large stained-glass hallway windows. Guests enjoy a comfortably furnished sitting room with lots of touristy brochures and interesting books on York and the surrounding villages. Bedrooms have received a complete renovation (1999), with new furniture, carpets, and linen. One is a family room, four are triples with a double and a twin bed, one is a single, and two are twins. Each has an en-suite bath or shower room, trouser press, satellite TV, and telephone. Dinner must be ordered by 4 pm of the same day. A ten-minute stroll finds you at York Minster, England's largest Gothic cathedral. Other attractions include the Jorvik Viking Museum, the Treasurer's House, the medieval streets of The Shambles with their inviting shops, and the castle with its adjacent museum. *Directions:* Take the A1237 (York North turnoff) from the A64 (the southern part of the York Outer Ring Road) to the A19 (signposted York City Centre). Go through the traffic lights at Clifton Green and when you see a footbridge going over the road, turn before it—this is St. Peter's Grove. Hobbits is at the end of the street on your left.

HOBBITS
Manager: Sandie McGlynn
9 St. Peter's Grove
York YO30 6AQ, England
Tel: (01904) 624538, Fax: (01904) 651765
E-mail: admin@ecsyork.co.uk
www.karenbrown.com/england/hobbits.html
8 rooms
£30 per person, dinner £10–£12
Open all year
Credit cards: MC, VS
Children welcome

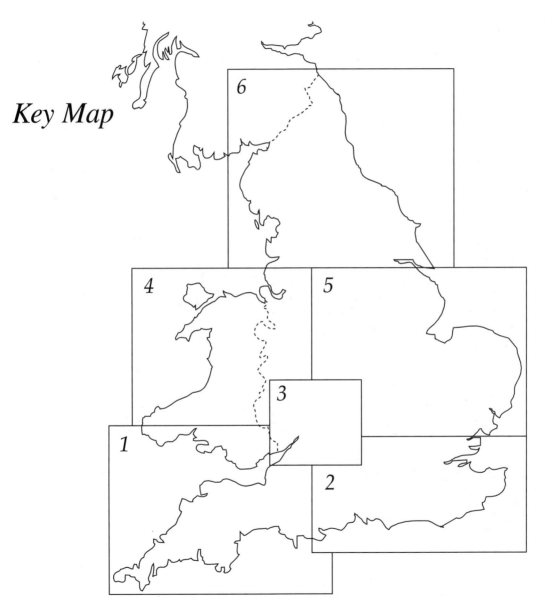

Key Map

6

4

5

3

1

2

Map 1

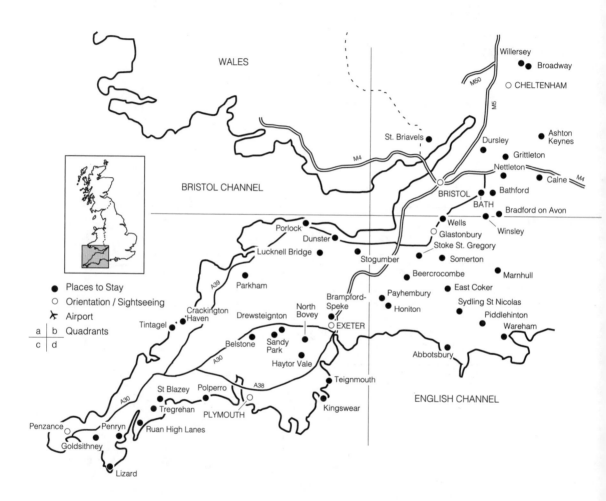

WALES

BRISTOL CHANNEL

Willersey
Broadway
○ CHELTENHAM

M50

M5

St. Briavels
Dursley
Ashton Keynes
Grittleton
Nettleton
Calne
M4

M4

○ BRISTOL
Bathford
BATH
Bradford on Avon
Wells
Glastonbury
Winsley
Porlock
Dunster
Stoke St. Gregory
Somerton
Lucknell Bridge
Stogumber
Beercrocombe
Marnhull
Parkham
East Coker
A39
Payhembury
Sydling St Nicolas
Brampford-Speke
Honiton
Piddlehinton
Wareham
Crackington Haven
Drewsteignton
North Bovey
Tintagel
○ EXETER
Belstone
Sandy Park
Haytor Vale
Abbotsbury
A30
A38
Teignmouth
St Blazey
Polperro
PLYMOUTH
Kingswear
ENGLISH CHANNEL
Tregrehan
A30
Penzance ○
Penryn
Ruan High Lanes
Goldsithney
Lizard

● Places to Stay
○ Orientation / Sightseeing
✈ Airport
Quadrants

a	b
c	d

Map 2

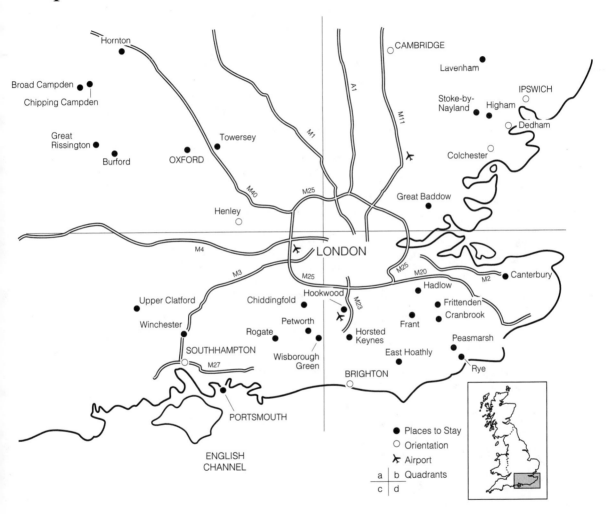

Hornton

Broad Campden
Chipping Campden

Great
Rissington
Burford

Towersey

OXFORD

Henley

Hornton

CAMBRIDGE

Lavenham

Stoke-by-
Nayland
Higham
IPSWICH

Dedham

Colchester

Great Baddow

A1

M11

M1

M40

M25

M4

M3

M25

M25

M20

M2

LONDON

Canterbury

Hadlow

Upper Clatford

Chiddingfold

Hookwood

Frittenden
Cranbrook

Winchester

Petworth

Frant

Rogate

Horsted
Keynes

Peasmarsh

SOUTHHAMPTON

Wisborough
Green

East Hoathly

Rye

M27

BRIGHTON

PORTSMOUTH

ENGLISH
CHANNEL

M23

● Places to Stay
○ Orientation
✈ Airport

| a | b | Quadrants |
| c | d | |

161

Map 3

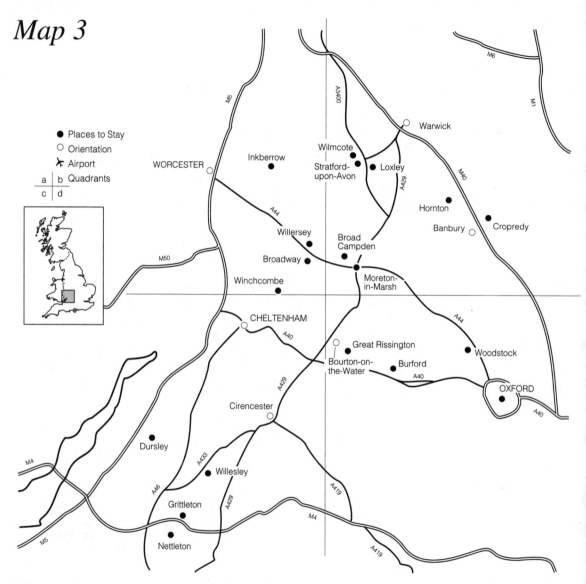

Legend:
- ● Places to Stay
- ○ Orientation
- ✈ Airport

a	b
c	d

Quadrants

Locations:

M6, M1, M5, A3400, Warwick, Wilmcote, Loxley, WORCESTER, Inkberrow, Stratford-upon-Avon, A429, M40, Hornton, A44, Banbury, Cropredy, Willersey, Broad Campden, Broadway, M50, Winchcombe, Moreton-in-Marsh, CHELTENHAM, A40, A44, Great Rissington, Woodstock, Bourton-on-the-Water, Burford, A429, A40, OXFORD, A40, Cirencester, Dursley, A433, M4, Willesley, A46, A429, Grittleton, M4, A419, Nettleton, M5, A419

Map 4

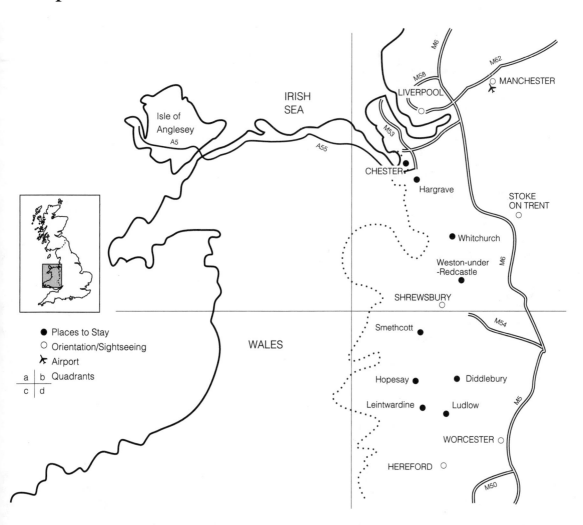

- ● Places to Stay
- ○ Orientation/Sightseeing
- ✈ Airport
- a | b
- c | d   Quadrants

IRISH SEA

Isle of Anglesey

A5

A55

LIVERPOOL

MANCHESTER

M6

M62

M58

M53

CHESTER

Hargrave

STOKE ON TRENT

Whitchurch

Weston-under -Redcastle

M6

SHREWSBURY

WALES

M54

Smethcott

Hopesay

Diddlebury

Leintwardine

Ludlow

M5

WORCESTER

HEREFORD

M50

Map 5

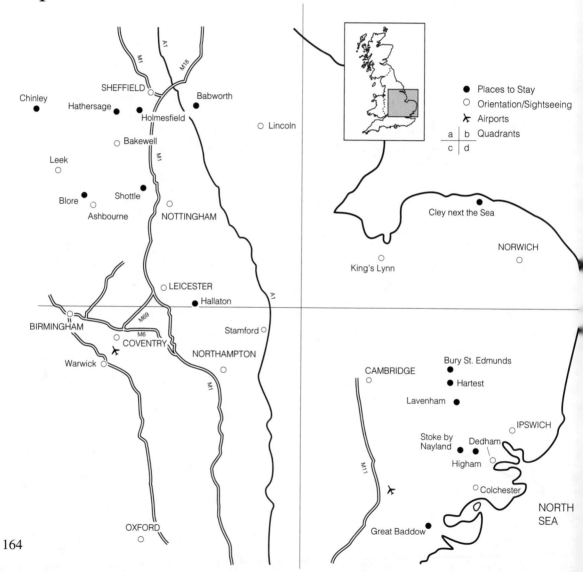

Chinley

Hathersage

SHEFFIELD

Babworth

Holmesfield

Lincoln

Bakewell

Leek

Blore

Shottle

Ashbourne

NOTTINGHAM

Cley next the Sea

NORWICH

King's Lynn

LEICESTER

Hallaton

BIRMINGHAM

Stamford

COVENTRY

NORTHAMPTON

Warwick

Bury St. Edmunds

CAMBRIDGE

Hartest

Lavenham

IPSWICH

Stoke by
Nayland

Dedham

Higham

Colchester

NORTH
SEA

OXFORD

Great Baddow

● Places to Stay
○ Orientation/Sightseeing
✈ Airports

| a | b | Quadrants |
| c | d | |

164

Map 6

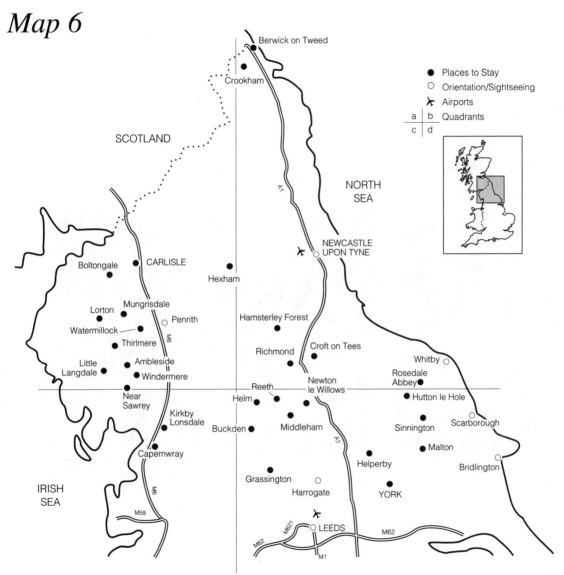

Berwick on Tweed
Crookham

SCOTLAND

NORTH SEA

● Places to Stay
○ Orientation/Sightseeing
✈ Airports
a | b
c | d Quadrants

Boltongale
CARLISLE
Hexham

NEWCASTLE UPON TYNE

Lorton
Mungrisdale
Penrith
Watermillock
Thirlmere

Hamsterley Forest

Croft on Tees
Whitby
Richmond
Rosedale Abbey

Little Langdale
Ambleside
Windermere

Reeth
Newton le Willows
Hutton le Hole

Near Sawrey
Helm

Kirkby Lonsdale
Buckden
Middleham
Sinnington
Scarborough
Malton

Capernwray

IRISH SEA

Grassington
Harrogate

Helperby
YORK
Bridlington

M58
M6
M62
M621
LEEDS
M1
M62

165

166

Places to Stay with Handicap Facilities

We list below all the places to stay that have ground-floor rooms or rooms specially equipped for the handicapped. Please discuss your requirements when you call your chosen place to stay to see if they have accommodation that is suitable for you.

Babworth, The Barns
Bath, Holly Lodge
Bath, Somerset House
Broad Campden, The Malt House
Cley next the Sea, Cley Mill Guest House
Croft on Tees, Clow Beck House
Crookham, The Coach House
Frittenden, Maplehurst Mill
Hargrave, Greenlooms Cottage
Hartest, The Hatch
Lorton, New House Farm
Loxley, Loxley Farm
Mungrisdale, The Mill Hotel

Near Sawrey, Ees Wyke Country House Hotel
Oxford, Cotswold House
Petworth, The Old Railway Station
Reeth, The Burgoyne Hotel
Richmond, Whashton Springs Farm
Shottle, Dannah Farm
Thirlmere, Dale Head Hall
Towersey, Upper Green Farm
Upper Clatford, Malt Cottage
Willersey, The Old Rectory
Wilmcote, Pear Tree Cottage
Windermere, Hawksmoor Guesthouse

Index

England, General Information (Introduction)
    Driving, 10
        Car Rental, 11
    Information Sources, 12
    Pubs, 13
    Shopping, 13
    Sightseeing, 14
    Weather, 14
Ennys Farm, Goldsithney, 61

F

Folly Hill Cottage, Cranbrook, 48
Fortitude Cottage, Portsmouth, 115
Fosse Farmhouse, Nettleton, 102
Frant
    The Old Parsonage, 59
Frittenden
    Maplehurst Mill, 60
Frog Street Farm, Beercrocombe, 23

G

Gate House, North Bovey, 105
Gold Court House, Wareham, 142
Goldsithney
    Ennys Farm, 61
Grasmead House, York, 157
Grassington
    Ashfield House, 62
Great Baddow
    Little Sir Hughes, 63
Great House, The, Lavenham, 87
Great Rissington
    The Lamb Inn, 64
Greenaway, Chiddingfold, 42
Greenlooms Cottage, Hargrave, 69
Grey Friar Lodge, Ambleside, 17
Grittleton
    Church House, 65

Grove House, Hamsterley Forest, 68

H

Hadlow
    Leavers Oast, 66
Hall, The, Newton le Willows, 103
Hallaton
    The Old Rectory, 67
Hammer and Hand, Hutton le Hole, 83
Hamsterley Forest
    Grove House, 68
Handicap Facilities List, 167
Hargrave
    Greenlooms Cottage, 69
Hartest
    The Hatch, 70
Hatch, The, Hartest, 70
Hathersage
    Carr Head Farm, 71
Hawksmoor Guest House, Windermere, 153
Haydon House, Bath, 19
Hayes Farmhouse, Peasmarsh, 109
Haytor Vale
    The Rock Inn, 72
Helm
    Helm Country House, 73
Helperby
    Brafferton Hall, 74
Hexham
    East Peterel Field Farm, 75
Higham
    The Old Vicarage, 76
Highlands Country House, Broadway, 32
Hipping Hall, Kirkby Lonsdale, 86
Hobbits, York, 158
Holly Lodge, Bath, 20
Holmesfield
    Horsleygate Hall, 77
Holmwood, Woodstock, 156

Index

Index   173

SHARE YOUR COMMENTS AND DISCOVERIES WITH US

Please share comments on properties that you have visited. We welcome accolades, as well as criticisms.

Also, we'd love to hear about any hotel or bed & breakfast you discover. Tell us what you liked about the property and, if possible, please include a brochure or photographs. We regret we cannot return photos.

Owner _____ Hotel or B&B _____

Address _____ Town _____ Country _____

Comments:

Your name _____ Street _____

Town _____ State _____ Zip _____ Country _____

Tel _____ E-mail _____ Date _____

Do we have your permission to electronically publish your comments on our website? Yes _____ No _____

If yes, would you like to remain anonymous? Yes ___No ___, or may we use your name? Yes___ No___

Please send report to: Karen Brown's Guides, Post Office Box 70, San Mateo, California 94401, USA
tel: (650) 342-9117, fax: (650) 342-9153, e-mail: karen@karenbrown.com, www.karenbrown.com

Become a Karen Brown Preferred Reader

Name _____

Street _____

Town _____

State _____ Zip _____ Country _____

Tel _____ Fax _____

E-mail _____

We'd love to welcome you as a Karen Brown Preferred Reader. Send us your name and address and you will be entered in our monthly drawing to receive a free set of Karen Brown guides. As a preferred reader, you will receive special promotions and be the first to know when new editions of Karen Brown guides go to press.

Please send to: Karen Brown's Guides, Post Office Box 70, San Mateo, California 94401, USA
tel: (650) 342-9117, fax: (650) 342-9153, e-mail: karen@karenbrown.com, website: www: karenbrown.com

Enhance Your Guides

Online

www.karenbrown.com

- Hotel News
- Color Photos
- New Discoveries
- Corrections & Edits
- Leisure Destinations
- Property of the Month
- Postcards from the Road
- Romantic Inns & Recipes

Visit Karen's Market

books, maps, itineraries
and travel accessories
selected with our
KB travelers in mind.

KB Travel Service

❖ **KB Travel Service** offers travel planning assistance using itineraries designed by *Karen Brown* and published in her guidebooks. We will customize any itinerary to fit your personal interests.

❖ We will plan your itinerary with you, help you decide how long to stay and what to do once you arrive, and work out the details.

❖ We will book your airline tickets and your rental car, arrange rail tickets or passes (including your seat reservations), reserve accommodations recommended in *Karen Brown's Guides,* and supply you with point-to-point information and consultation.

Contact us to start planning your travel!

800 782-2128 ext. 328 or e-mail: info@kbtravelservice.com

Service fees do apply

KB Travel Service
16 East Third Avenue
San Mateo, CA 94401 USA
www.kbtravelservice.com

Independently owned and operated by Town & Country Travel
CST 2001543-10

is the

Preferred Airline

of

Karen Brown's Guides

auto europe®

Karen Brown's

Preferred Car Rental Service Provider

for

Worldwide Car Rental Services
Chauffeur & Transfer Services
Prestige & Sports Cars
Motor Home Rentals

1-800-223-5555

Be sure to identify yourself as a Karen Brown Traveler.
For special offers and discounts use your
Karen Brown ID number 99006187.

Seal Cove Inn

Located in the San Francisco Bay Area

Karen Brown Herbert (best known as author of the Karen Brown's guides) and her husband, Rick, have put 22 years of experience into reality and opened their own superb hideaway, Seal Cove Inn. Spectacularly set amongst wild flowers and bordered by towering cypress trees, Seal Cove Inn looks out to the distant ocean over acres of county park: an oasis where you can enjoy secluded beaches, explore tidepools, watch frolicking seals, and follow the tree-lined path that traces the windswept ocean bluffs. Country antiques, original watercolors, flower-laden cradles, rich fabrics, and the gentle ticking of grandfather clocks create the perfect ambiance for a foggy day in front of the crackling log fire. Each bedroom is its own haven with a cozy sitting area before a wood-burning fireplace and doors opening onto a private balcony or patio with views to the park and ocean. Moss Beach is a 35-minute drive south of San Francisco, 6 miles north of the picturesque town of Half Moon Bay, and a few minutes from Princeton harbor with its colorful fishing boats and restaurants. Seal Cove Inn makes a perfect base for whale-watching, salmon-fishing excursions, day trips to San Francisco, exploring the coast, or, best of all, just a romantic interlude by the sea, time to relax and be pampered. Karen and Rick look forward to the pleasure of welcoming you to their coastal hideaway.

Seal Cove Inn • 221 Cypress Avenue • Moss Beach • California • 94038 • USA
tel: (650) 728-4114, fax: (650) 728-4116, e-mail: sealcove@coastside.net, website: sealcoveinn.com

TRAVELSMITH®

Need a dual voltage hair dryer, a wrinkle-free blazer, quick-dry clothes, a computer adapter plug? TRAVELSMITH has them all, along with an enticing array of everything a Karen Brown traveler needs.

Karen Brown recommends TRAVELSMITH as an excellent source for travel clothing and gear. We were pleased to find quality products needed for our own research travels in their catalog—items not always easy to find. For a free catalog call TRAVELSMITH at 800-950-1600.

When placing your order, be sure to identify yourself as a Karen Brown Traveler with the code TKB99 and you will receive a 10% discount*. You can link to TRAVELSMITH through our website *www.karenbrown.com*.

*offer valid till December 2000

Travel Your Dreams • Order your Karen Brown Guides Today

Please ask in your local bookstore for Karen Brown's Guides. If the books you want are unavailable, you may order directly from the publisher. Books will be shipped immediately.

_____ *Austria: Charming Inns & Itineraries* $18.95

_____ *California: Charming Inns & Itineraries* $18.95

_____ *England: Charming Bed & Breakfasts* $17.95

_____ *England, Wales & Scotland: Charming Hotels & Itineraries* $18.95

_____ *France: Charming Bed & Breakfasts* $17.95

_____ *France: Charming Inns & Itineraries* $18.95

_____ *Germany: Charming Inns & Itineraries* $18.95

_____ *Ireland: Charming Inns & Itineraries* $18.95

_____ *Italy: Charming Bed & Breakfasts* $17.95

_____ *Italy: Charming Inns & Itineraries* $18.95

_____ *Portugal: Charming Inns & Itineraries* $18.95

_____ *Spain: Charming Inns & Itineraries* $18.95

_____ *Switzerland: Charming Inns & Itineraries* $18.95

Name _____ Street _____

Town _____ State _____ Zip _____ Tel _____

Credit Card (MasterCard or Visa) _____ Expires: _____

For orders in the USA, add $4 for the first book and $1 for each additional book for shipment. California residents add 8.25% sales tax. Overseas orders add $10 per book for airmail shipment. Indicate number of copies of each title; fax or mail form with check or credit card information to:

KAREN BROWN'S GUIDES
Post Office Box 70 • San Mateo • California • 94401 • USA
tel: (650) 342-9117, fax: (650) 342-9153, e-mail: karen@karenbrown.com
You can also order directly from our website at www.karenbrown.com.

KAREN BROWN wrote her first travel guide in 1976. Her personalized travel series has grown to thirteen titles which Karen and her small staff work diligently to keep updated. Karen, her husband, Rick, and their children, Alexandra and Richard, live in Moss Beach, a small town on the coast south of San Francisco. They settled here in 1991 when they opened Seal Cove Inn. Karen is frequently traveling, but when she is home, in her role as innkeeper, enjoys welcoming Karen Brown readers.

CLARE BROWN, CTC, was a travel consultant for many years, specializing in planning itineraries to Europe using charming small hotels in the countryside. The focus of her job remains unchanged, but now her expertise is available to a larger audience—the readers of her daughter Karen's country inn guides. When Clare and her husband, Bill, are not traveling, they live either in Hillsborough, California, or at their home in Vail, Colorado, where family and friends frequently join them for skiing.

JUNE BROWN'S love of travel was inspired by the *National Geographic* magazines that she read as a girl in her dentist's office—so far she has visited over 40 countries. June hails from Sheffield, England and lived in Zambia and Canada before moving to northern California where she lives in San Mateo with her husband, Tony, their daughter Clare, their German Shepherd, and a Siamese cat.

BARBARA TAPP, the talented artist who produces all of the hotel sketches and delightful illustrations in this guide, was raised in Australia where she studied in Sydney at the School of Interior Design. Although Barbara continues with freelance projects, she devotes much of her time to illustrating the Karen Brown guides. Barbara lives in Kensington, California, with her husband, Richard, their two sons, Jonothan and Alexander, and daughter, Georgia.

JANN POLLARD, the artist responsible for the beautiful painting on the cover of this guide, has studied art since childhood, and is well-known for her outstanding impressionistic-style watercolors which she has exhibited in numerous juried shows, winning many awards. Jann travels frequently to Europe (using Karen Brown's guides) where she loves to paint historical buildings. Jann lives in Burlingame, California, with her husband, Gene.